CW01665233

The Pan-African Plant-Based Alliance

FROM SOIL TO SOUL:

AFRICAN VEGAN

RECIPES

An inspiring fusion of Pan-Africanism and plant-based lifestyles

Global Book Publishing

From Soil to Soul
The Pan-African Plant-Based Alliance
©2024 The Pan-African Plant-Based Alliance.
All rights reserved.

All rights reserved. No part of this publication may be reproduced, distributed, or transmitted in any form or by any means, including photocopying, recording, or other electronic or mechanical methods, without the prior written permission of the author or publisher (except by a reviewer, who may quote brief passages and/or show brief video clips in a review).

ISBN: 978-1-964644-18-9
Book Design & Publishing done by:
Global Book Publishing
www.globalbookpublishing.com

Disclaimer: The Publisher and the Authors make no representations or warranties with respect to the accuracy and completeness of this work and specially disclaim all warranties, including without limitation warranties of fitness for a particular purpose. No warranty may be created or extended by sales or promotional materials. The advice and strategies contain herein may not be suitable for every situation. This work is sold with the understanding that the Publisher is not engaged in rendering legal, accounting, or other professional services. If professional assistance is required, the services of a competent professional person should be sought. Neither the Publisher nor the Author shall be liable for the damages arising here from. The fact that an organization or website is referred to in this work as a citation or potential source of further information does not mean that the Author or the Publisher endorses the information the organization or the website may provide or recommendations it may make. Further, readers should be aware that internet websites listed in this work may have changed or disappeared between when this work was written and when it is used.

This book is dedicated to the global family of African descent in Africa and beyond. In the spirit of Pan-Africanism, guided by Maat principles, Ubuntu wisdom, and the ethics of Veganism, let this cookbook be a culinary bridge that unites us all.

TABLE OF CONTENTS

INTRODUCTION

At the heart of this cookbook lies an inspiring fusion of two compelling themes: the power of plant-based eating and the celebration of Pan-Africanism.

This cookbook aims to inspire Afro descendent to embrace the richness of a plant-based lifestyle while reconnecting with their African heritage and embracing the principles of Pan-Africanism.

By celebrating traditional African dishes, we seek to ignite a sense of pride and belonging in people of African descent, on and off the continent. We strive to demonstrate that plant-based eating is not a limitation but a gateway to a world of unlimited culinary adventures compatible with African cuisines.

By highlighting the interconnectedness of all living beings, as emphasized in Ubuntu philosophy, and by embodying the principles of justice, ethics, and moral integrity represented by Maat, we encourage readers to delve even deeper into the ethical and cultural dimensions of their food choices.

In doing so, we hope to cultivate a culinary bridge that unites and elevates us all, from the richness of our soil to the depth of our souls.

Hotep!

Now let's get into the basics. So, who are we?

We are the **Pan-African Plant-Based Alliance (PPBA)**, an international non-profit organisation. We are on a mission to bring a self-sufficient plant-based food system back to Africa and inspire the African diaspora to go plant-based while embracing their African heritage. The PPBA was created in 2023 by **Stéphane Kotto** – born and raised in Cameroon.

What is the PPBA vision?

A united and self-sufficient Africa and diaspora that thrives on delicious, healthy, sustainable, accessible, and affordable plant-based food.

What is the PPBA mission?

With the threat of factory farms rising across the continent, our mission is clear: bring a self-sufficient plant-based food system back to Africa. We aim to do this by inspiring African people on and off the continent to go and stay plant-based. We also want to build a community of African businesses, industry experts, investors, policymakers, educational institutions, medical institutions, and like-minded NGOs to develop a plant-based food system in Africa.

Why is the PPBA doing this?

Our reasons are simple:

1. For the well-being and prosperity of African people and the diaspora
2. For the Motherland and our planet
3. For ethics, justice, and integrity

Now that we've established the basics, let's get into some specifics about our values.

- **Pan-Africanism**

  Pan-Africanism is a philosophy and a global movement dedicated to fostering self-love, love, solidarity, cooperation, integrity, dignity, self-determination, and unity among people of African descent around the world. Its vision is to achieve a collective sovereignty and prosperity, allowing everyone to thrive in harmony with the rest of humanity.

  Instead of advocating for further integration into oppressive systems, both on and off the African continent, Pan-Africanism promotes self-determination and champions an independent, sovereign, self-sufficient system, free from external control, and domination. It addresses social, cultural, economical, geopolitical, and environmental issues to ensure the sovereignty, well-being, and prosperity of all people of African descent.

This philosophy extends to both those who live on the African continent and those in the African diaspora around the world, transcending boundaries of nationality, ethnicity, tribes, religion, skin tones, sexual orientation, or gender.

At its core, Pan-Africanism is grounded in the belief that, despite our differences, people of African descent share deep cultural, social, spiritual, and historical roots.

No matter our place of birth or language spoken, whether in Africa, Europe, America, or the Caribbean, we must embrace our shared African identity.

As branches of the same tree, we are united by the same roots and our destinies are thus intricately intertwined.

Contrary to popular narratives, it is crucial to recognise that our roots extend beyond the trauma of slavery and colonisation. In Ancient Egypt, our ancestors pioneered modern civilisation, advancing knowledge in various fields from astrophysics, mathematics, and medicine to art, spirituality, and philosophy.

As Jamaican Pan-African Marcus Garvey once said, "*A people without knowledge of their past history, origin and culture is like a tree without roots*".

Understanding and embracing our rich history is essential for our community as it fosters cultural identity, builds unity, and provides valuable lessons from the past, guiding the community towards a brighter future.

More than a concept, Pan-Africanism compels us to champion a collective unity to address challenges related to systemic racism and neocolonialism, aiming to achieve the total liberation of our global community.

It is a movement that beckons us to cast aside the shadows of division to focus on the brilliant light that emanates when we stand united.

At the Pan-African Plant-Based Alliance, we advocate for a world where all people of African origin, on every continent, are united, self-sufficient, and proud.

- **Ubuntu**

  One of the foundations of Pan-African thinking is the concept of Ubuntu. It is a traditional African philosophy that emphasises the interconnectedness of all living beings. It emphasises the significance of community and compassion within the intricate web of life that envelops us all. It is often translated as "I am because you are". In other words, all human or non-human beings have inherent value and deserve to be respected and honoured.

  Ubuntu encapsulates the belief in shared humanity echoes through the spirit of Pan-Africanism. It invites us to recognise the intrinsic worth of every individual, acknowledging that our destinies are interwoven. As we embrace a plant-based lifestyle, let it be a testament to our commitment to the well-being of not just ourselves, but all living beings.

- **Maat**

  We are sure this is a term that fellow ancient history nerds are familiar with. Maat is a guiding principle from Kemet, the Ancient Black-African Egyptian civilisation before the Ottomans, Romans, and Greeks invaded.

  Maat is the goddess and personification of justice, truth, harmony, cosmic order, and the balance of nature. It is an African philosophy that guides personal and social behaviour, emphasising the importance of leading a life with integrity and honourable moral conduct. In the spirit of Maat, let our choices be a beacon of justice, integrity, and harmony, shining light on the path towards a liberated future.

- **Veganism**

  This word often triggers certain sentiments as it's a word that is often misunderstood, so let's clarify it.

  Veganism is defined as a lifestyle that seeks to exclude, **as far as possible and practicable**, all forms of exploitation of and cruelty to, non-human animals for food, fashion, research, entertainment, and any other purpose.

  While the word vegan was coined back in 1944, avoiding unnecessary harm to non-human animals is not a Western trend. It is rooted in ancient moral philosophies across the world since the beginning of civilisation in Africa. In Kemet, for instance, the 42 Laws of Maat included the directive "thou shalt not kill". This moral principle, written thousands of years ago and shared across many religions, suggests that life should not be taken needlessly – a concept perfectly aligned with veganism.

  In short, veganism is simply based on the idea that non-human animals should have the right to live and to be free regardless of their species. A concept transcending boundaries of race, gender, generations, religion, social class, and politics.

  Moreover, it challenges the notion that non-human animals are commodities, objects, or properties that can be owned, exploited, and traded due to their non-human status.

  Ok, but what's the difference between vegetarian and plant-based lifestyles?

  A vegetarian lifestyle refers to a diet that does not consume any land or marine animals, but includes animal-derived products like dairy, eggs, or honey.

  A plant-based lifestyle simply refers to a diet that focuses exclusively on plant-based food. Often perceived as exclusive, it is quite the opposite as it is the only diet everyone can enjoy regardless of diet preferences or religious beliefs.

  Various factors contribute to these two lifestyles, including health and environmental benefits, spiritual and religious beliefs, or personal taste preferences.

  On the other hand, as explained previously, veganism goes beyond diet and focuses on our relationship with non-human animals.

In the spirit of Pan-Africanism, Ubuntu, and Maat, the Pan-African Plant-Based Alliance promotes veganism for ethics, justice, and integrity and a plant-based diet for the well-being and prosperity of our global community, our motherland, and the planet. These principles are at the core of everything our organisation does and in every recipe in this cookbook. As we embark on a journey towards plant-based living across the motherland, let us nourish our bodies and collective souls.

Reasons to Consider a Plant-Based Diet for Our Health

Common health issues such as Type 2 diabetes, heart disease, high blood pressure, strokes, and various cancers are prevalent in our society. Unfortunately, these diseases are the leading causes of death in Africa and among the diaspora.

Amidst a global health crisis, hospitals are facing unprecedented levels of activity. While some traditional health systems address root causes, most modern systems focus on managing symptoms, leading to a reliance on medications that primarily benefit pharmaceutical businesses and perpetuate a cycle of illness and profit.

One frequently overlooked factor is our dietary choices, particularly the consumption of animal products. Despite the widespread belief that eating animals, drinking their milk, or consuming their eggs is 'natural', 'normal', and 'necessary', it prompts us to question whether this assumption truly holds merit.

Do we need to consume animal meat in order to be healthy?

The idea that consuming animals is essential for optimal health is challenged by the historical evidence of civilisations that have thrived on vegetarian and plant-based diets for centuries. Throughout history, various cultures across Asia, the Middle East, and Africa have been abstaining from eating animals, demonstrating that a balanced and nutritious diet can be sustained without relying on meat. It is through colonisation that we learned to eat this much meat.

Despite this fact, there is still a common belief that our health depends on consuming animals, usually to get proteins, although all proteins originate from plants. The planet's most robust creatures, such as elephants, rhinos, and gorillas, thrive on plant-based diets. Instead of relying on animals as a middleman, why not get protein directly from the source?

Beyond ethical and environmental considerations, this approach offers health benefits by avoiding LDL cholesterol – the 'bad' cholesterol exclusive to animals. Accumulation of LDL cholesterol can lead to arterial blockages, increasing the risk of conditions like type 2 diabetes, heart disease, and high blood pressure, regardless of animal welfare standards.

The World Health Organisation (WHO), after reviewing over 800 studies from 10 countries, categorises processed meat like sausages, bacon, nuggets, and salami, as a Group 1 carcinogen, placing it alongside cigarettes, asbestos, and plutonium. This underscores the significant health risks associated with consuming processed meat.

What about fish? Don't we need omega-3?

While fish is part of many traditional African dishes and is a source of omega-3, it is important to note that we do not need fish to get omega-3. Just like cows get their proteins by eating plants, fish get their omega-3 by eating algae. These fatty acids move up the food chain as smaller fish consume the algae. Larger fish, in turn, eat smaller fish, accumulating higher concentrations of omega-3 fatty acids.

So why not skip the middleman and get our omega-3 directly from plants?

This way, we avoid the saturated fat and LDL cholesterol as well as the toxic polychlorinated biphenyls (PCBs), mercury, and microplastics that accumulate in fish flesh due to ocean pollution.

Fortunately, seaweed and algae, flaxseeds, pumpkin seeds, chia seeds, hemp seeds, or walnuts are rich in omega-3s, and provide a healthier alternative.

Could consuming animals lead to another pandemic?

The use of antibiotics in factory farming and fish farms, driven by the demand for meat, dairy, eggs, and fish, is fuelling a global crisis – antibiotic resistance. This risky practice, widespread in both the West and Africa, not only jeopardises our health by introducing resistant bacteria through animal products but also creates a breeding ground for dangerous viruses.

Consuming these animal products contributes to the development of antibiotic-resistant bacteria in our bodies, posing severe health risks. The WHO warns that antibiotic resistance is a major threat, causing over 700,000 deaths annually and projected to surpass 10 million deaths yearly by 2050. Without changing our food system, the next pandemic isn't a matter of if, but when.

But didn't our ancestors eat meat?

Yes and no, as indicated by recent research, including studies published in Nature Ecology & Evolution. The current understanding suggests that early humans predominantly relied on a plant-based diet, consisting of fruits, vegetables, and nuts, much like many primates today. Their occasional consumption of animals was driven by survival needs when plant resources were scarce. In contrast, today's dietary choices for many revolve more around taste pleasure than survival necessity.

Okay, but aren't we biologically designed to kill and consume animals?

In contrast to true omnivores and carnivores with sharp teeth designed for hunting, our small and flat teeth lack the natural attributes needed for killing prey.

Practically speaking, our teeth aren't suited for dispatching farm animals like cows, pigs, sheep, or chickens. Unlike carnivores and omnivores equipped for such tasks, we rely on tools to slaughter, cut, and cook our food. Rather than being designed for tearing flesh, our canine teeth assist in tearing hard fruits, nuts, and vegetables – a trait shared with other primates.

Adding to the distinction, our jaw structure allows for side-to-side movement during chewing, unlike natural carnivores and omnivores whose jaws move up and down to tear and swallow flesh. Lacking claws and featuring small, harmless nails, we stand in contrast to true carnivores and omnivores.

Furthermore, our intestinal length, ranging between 7 and 13 times the length of our torso, aligns more with herbivores and frugivores, rather than carnivores or omnivores. Unlike these animals, whose shorter intestines swiftly process animal flesh, our longer intestines make us susceptible to health issues like type 2 diabetes and heart diseases when regularly consuming animals.

Unlike omnivores or carnivores, humans lack an inherent killing instinct for hunting and eating animals. Unlike carnivore or omnivore babies, a human baby doesn't instinctively hunt, kill, and eat animals.

In summary, while our behaviour aligns with omnivores, our physiology leans more towards that of natural plant-eaters.

But how can I get enough vitamin B12 without consuming animals?

While plants offer a comprehensive array of nutrients, there's one exception to note: Vitamin B12. This essential vitamin isn't sourced from plants or animals but originates from bacteria in cobalt-rich soils and water. While it used to be naturally present in plants before the industrial era, modern sanitation processes eliminate all traces of B12 from plants. As a result, it's advisable for both farmed animals and humans, irrespective of dietary choices, to consider B12 supplements.

Don't I need milk and cheese for calcium?

First, like any mammal, let's remember that the only milk we ever needed is our mothers', as babies. Past that point, we no longer need to consume milk from humans, and we certainly don't need to consume milk from other species.

While many believe in the necessity of cow's milk for calcium and strong bones, its consumption poses significant health risks. Like any animal products, cow's milk is not only high in LDL cholesterol, but also in hormones like oestrogens, which increases the risk of chronic diseases such as diabetes, heart issues, and hormone-related cancers.

Despite over 90% of the Black population being lactose intolerant, dairy consumption is rising in Africa and within the diaspora. This is primarily due to the consumption of cheese, whose addiction can be attributed to casomorphin, a substance that drives infants to desire their mother's milk.

Ultimately, cow's milk is designed for baby cows; thus, it is unnecessary for humans. Spinach, broccoli, or kale are great sources of calcium, while plant-based alternatives, such as soy, cashews, almonds, oats, or rice, offer a similar taste to milk, without the negative health consequences. So you've got to ask yourself, are you a baby cow?

What about eggs?

Eggs are often considered a healthier choice among all animal products, but is this true? Whether fertilised or not, an egg is designed to sustain a developing chicken for 21 days without external energy. Consequently, eggs are rich in saturated fat and cholesterol, increasing the risk of type 2 diabetes and heart disease. Moreover, eggs contain hormones like oestrogens, produced in the hen ovaries, which, like milk, can disrupt our hormonal balance and elevate the risk of hormone-related diseases.

Does consuming animal products guarantee the development of these diseases?

Certainly not. Just as some individuals can smoke their entire lives without developing lung cancer, while others may develop it even after a short period of smoking, the risk varies for each person. It's a matter of individual susceptibility.

Contrary to common beliefs, the encouraging aspect is that many of these diseases are not purely genetic. Often, they are prevalent among relatives due to shared dietary and lifestyle choices. By addressing the underlying causes, we have the potential not only to heal but also to thrive.

Why hasn't my doctor told me all of this?

In our capitalist society, the focus on treatment over prevention prevails, primarily benefiting the pharmaceutical industry, a powerful global lobby. While treatment is vital, our society tends to treat sick patients rather than preventing illness. Medical education often prioritises teaching symptom management with medications, overlooking the crucial role of nutrition.

This system leads individuals with chronic diseases to rely on multiple medications, despite evidence that a well-balanced whole food plant-based diet can prevent and reverse some of these diseases. Unfortunately, the promotion of animal products persists through various channels, including government guidelines, schools, and hospitals, neglecting the potential of healthier dietary choices. We can do better.

So what defines the perfect diet?

While there's no one-size-fits-all solution, some plant-based diets prove better than others. Generally, less-processed diets, especially a well-balanced whole food plant-based diet, stand out as optimal for human health.

Food is crucial for health, but it's not the sole factor. Seeking professional advice, especially for specific conditions, is advised. Conducting personal research empowers us to make informed choices.

But isn't plant-based food expensive and hard to find?

Contrary to popular belief, it's the most affordable and widely accessible food globally, especially staples like corn, rice, beans, cassava, millet, fonio, potatoes, plantains, or lentils, commonly consumed by less-privileged populations. Notably, alternatives to meat, dairy, and eggs might seem pricier on average due to subsidies for animal products, but they are usually more economical than high-quality organic animal products.

The quote 'Let food be thy medicine and medicine be thy food', often attributed to Ancient Greek Hippocrates, traces its roots to Imhotep, the father of modern medicine, who practised in Kemet thousands of years before Hippocrates.

So with this quote in mind, let the recipes in this cookbook guide you to better health!

Reasons to Consider a Plant-Based Diet for Our Motherland and Our Planet

The African population, currently the world's fastest-growing, is expected to double by 2050 and exceed 4 billion by the century's end. While demographic challenges exist, Western advice to limit childbirth for environmental reasons oversimplifies this complex issue.

Despite having 4 times more people, Africa's contribution to greenhouse gas emissions is a fraction of that of the United States, highlighting that population growth isn't the sole concern. Collective lifestyle choices play a crucial role, particularly in the food system. Research shows that *even if fossil fuel emissions stop immediately, emissions from our food systems alone could increase global temperatures by more than 1.5°C*. This highlights the necessity of transforming our food system to avoid more intense and frequent extreme weather events, further water shortages, droughts, and food scarcities affecting hundreds of millions on the continent and within the diaspora. Failure to do so could force people into becoming climate refugees, creating further conflicts and further challenges to the development of the continent.

Historically, the demand for animal products in Africa increased during colonisation and persists with neocolonial influences, promoting Western-style, animal-heavy diets. This trend threatens traditional, affordable, plant-based African dishes.

Consequently, large-scale intensive factory farms are emerging across the continent, posing a threat to meeting current and future needs. If current trends persist, meat consumption is projected to increase by 30% in 2030, with the farmed animal population in Africa expected to surge from 2.6 billion in 2012 to 9.4 billion in 2050, surpassing all Western nations combined.

Deciding which food system is therefore crucial for the continent from an environmental, social, economic, and geopolitical point of view.

Can Western-style factory farms offer a solution for Africa?

Originating in the West in the mid-20th century to meet post-war demands for animal products, these concentrated animal feeding operations (CAFOs) have become a dominant source in the West and are increasingly seen as a solution to meet the rising demand for affordable animal products in African cities.

Despite initially addressing food security, factory farming has now become a major contributor to environmental degradation globally, impacting public health, livelihoods, and causing unimaginable animal suffering. The United Nations (UN) reports that *the global consumption of meat, fish, dairy, and eggs emits more greenhouse gases than all of the cars, trucks, boats, trains, and planes in the world, combined annually.*

One primary factor contributing to this issue is the extensive land and water resources required for animal agriculture.

Currently, over 80% of global farmland is dedicated to this purpose, yet animal agriculture provides less than 20% of all calories and less than 40% of all the protein consumed in the world. The growing demand for animal products further exacerbates this issue, leading to wasteful land and water consumption.

As a result, rainforests are being set on fire primarily to graze cattle or grow crops like soy, to then feed billions of animals worldwide.

Consequently, factory farming is the leading cause of deforestation, which releases even more carbon dioxide, accelerating global warming. This also leads to further species extinctions and endangers indigenous tribes who have coexisted harmoniously with these lands for centuries. *Isn't it a form of colonisation?*

Moreover, raising more cattle also means more methane emissions, a greenhouse gas over 25 times more powerful than CO_2, which is released through the ruminant's digestive system, thus accelerating global warming.

Introducing factory farms in Africa would therefore exacerbate health and environmental issues, leading to food insecurity and reliance on imports. From a geopolitical standpoint, it may hinder Africa's pursuit of self-sufficiency, potentially compromising its independence from Western and BRIC countries.

In conclusion, aside from ethical concerns, embracing factory farms in Africa would bring about additional health and environmental challenges, negatively impacting the continent's future and self-sufficiency.

What about animal products from local farms? Are they not more sustainable than buying plant food from abroad?

Well, not according to science. When it comes to beef, only 0.5% of emissions come from transportation, and for lamb, it's only 2%. In fact, for most food products, transportation accounts for less than 10%, as they are typically transported via boats. This means that the primary issue lies in the farming itself.

Moreover, aside from ethical and health concerns, relying solely on small local farms poses challenges in meeting the growing demand, requiring an increase in the number of animals. This is precisely why the West adopted factory farm systems in the first place. Following the law of supply and demand, this system would inevitably raise the price of animal products, making them accessible only to the privileged few and exacerbating existing inequalities.

What about regenerative agriculture? Isn't that beneficial for the environment?

Regenerative agriculture, also known as 'holistic management', is being promoted by the meat industry as a way for grazing cattle to absorb carbon back into the soil. However, studies show that this only offsets 20–60% of the emissions produced by the animals. After a few decades, the soil can't absorb more carbon, making the strategy ineffective. This may lead farmers to expand grazing land, causing deforestation or stopping farming altogether.

In short, whether it's factory farms, local meat, small farms, or regenerative agriculture, none of these methods ensures a sustainable food system for Africa, as they don't meet current needs without harming the ability of future generations.

What about fish and seafood?

In response to the increasing demand for fish, three-fourths of the world's fisheries are already overexploited or significantly depleted, particularly in African waters exploited by Western and Chinese vessels. This leaves local fishermen, who rely on fish for survival, with limited opportunities. The bottom-trolling fishing method alone produces emissions equivalent to the entire aviation industry.

Globally, humans annually destroy nearly 4 billion acres of sea beds to feed themselves and for animal feed, which is about 15 times more than land deforestation. African waters, crucial for capturing CO_2 and providing oxygen, are under increasing threat. *A study warns of fishless oceans by 2048 if no action is taken.*

While fish farming is growing in Africa to meet demand, it brings ethical and health concerns. Similar to land animal farming, fish farms require substantial feed, often sourced from captured fish or plant-based alternatives that could be used for human consumption, leading to food and water waste. Fish farms also contribute to the risk of a global antibiotic resistance pandemic, as antibiotics are used in crowded conditions. As previously discussed, according to the WHO, antibiotic resistance is a major threat to global health and food security.

Non-industrial fishing faces similar challenges and cannot meet the growing demand on its own. Relying solely on small-scale fishing would likely increase fish prices, exacerbating inequalities due to the law of supply and demand.

So, what can we do about all of this?

A meta-analysis involving 1530 research papers found that if we switch to a plant-based way of eating, *we can feed an additional 4 billion people and use 75% less farmland. That's like freeing up an area as big as Australia, China, the EU, and the United States combined!* While some communities might need animal products, for most people, we don't have to raise animals for food. We could use all that land to grow affordable and tasty plant-based food in a sustainable way, which can reduce hunger and create jobs across our global community.

While we primarily promote local and indigenous African plant-based food relevant to each country, innovative and realistic meat and seafood alternatives made in Africa from locally sourced plants are not a necessity but a good complimentary option for people who enjoy the taste of animal products, but do not want to contribute to its negative impact.

Soy, peas, wheat, or fava beans are great crops to create meaty textures when blended and mixed with the right spices, but also cashew, lentils, jackfruits, banana blossoms, or mushrooms, which are great to create natural, unprocessed realistic meat and seafood alternatives with the right seasoning.

While some of these options are not widely developed yet, they are still available in parts of Africa and have significantly fewer negative impacts than animal products.

But it's not just about producing what we need; it's also about fixing and restoring our broken relationship with the natural world.

The rest of the land could be used to restore rainforests, wildlife, healthy ecosystems, and capture carbon dioxide, which is key. This could help to significantly reduce greenhouse gas emissions, deforestation, and save more land and water. Plus, it could prevent wild animals and local indigenous tribes from disappearing, which is key to preserving African ancestral knowledge.

In addition to reducing animal exploitation and suffering, reintroducing a plant-based food system to Africa could enhance overall self-sufficiency, meeting the population's needs without jeopardising future generations' well-being. Afterall, this is precisely what Maat is about: justice, integrity, balance, and harmony between humans, non-human animals, and the natural world.

Reasons to Embrace a Vegan Lifestyle

This takes us to the eye-roll-inducing word ‘veganism’ we previously defined. While many individuals claim to be against animal cruelty, it’s common for people to contribute to harm unknowingly. Despite caring about animals’ well-being, our food choices often indirectly or directly cause their suffering and death. This isn’t to label anyone as ‘bad’ but to raise awareness about the impact of our choices on non-human animals. The intention is not to pass judgement or induce guilt but to encourage making food choices in line with personal values, traditions, and cultures.

How can we claim to oppose something while supporting it every day?

When it comes to eating animals, many of us grapple with cognitive dissonance – the mental discomfort of holding conflicting beliefs. While we profess a belief in respecting animal well-being, our actions of killing them for taste pleasure contradicts this ideal, creating what is known as the meat paradox.

Living in societies that shield us from the reality of animal farming, we are fed a fairy tale of idyllic farms through adverts, packaging, and even children’s media. We’ve altered our language to avoid discomfort, distancing meat from its origin. We say ‘beef’ or ‘steak’, not cows; we say ‘pork’ or ‘sausages’, not pigs; and we say ‘meat’, not ‘body parts’, although this is what meat is about in the first place.

Yet, when we do confront the process, the humane narrative often unravels. Once arrived at the slaughterhouse, animals are so frightened that they often try to escape as they can smell the blood and hear the screams of others. Unfortunately for them, this facility is specifically designed to make sure they don’t come out alive.

While the religious ways avoid stunning the animals, the standard non-religious practice involves stunning before slaughter. They are either electrocuted, shot in the head via a captive bolt gun which perforates their skull, or locked up in a gas chamber. Upon losing consciousness, though they frequently regain awareness, they are then hung upside down so workers can slit their throats and behead them. Regardless of the method chosen, can we truly label it ‘humane’ to unnecessarily kill someone who would rather live?

To avoid answering this question, we like to tell ourselves that we shouldn’t use the word ‘someone’ since they are not humans. However, if they are not someone, what are they, something?

Sadly, this fate befalls over 3.8 billion animals daily worldwide, constituting the largest massacre in history, by far. *To give some perspective, if a ‘higher’ species would treat us the way we treat animals, the human race would go extinct in less than 2 days.*

Irrespective of their welfare standards, most farmed animals face the same gruesome end. Many people unaware of these realities may choose vegetarianism, yet this alone doesn’t spare animals from this unimaginable suffering, as dairy cows for cheese and hens for eggs are sent to slaughterhouses when they are no longer profitable. In addition, both male baby cows and male baby chicks are killed since they cannot produce milk and eggs.

To alleviate cognitive dissonance, aligning our behaviour with our belief in respecting animal well-being necessitates a shift towards veganism. This lifestyle seeks to exclude, *as far as possible and practicable*, all forms of exploitation and cruelty to non-human animals for food, clothing, and any other purpose.

Does being vegan mean causing no harm at all?

Certainly not, as simply being alive can inadvertently result in harm, even in the cultivation of certain crops. However, conscious intent matters. Distinguishing between purposeful harm and accidental harm. For instance, there's a clear distinction between accidentally hitting a dog on the road and deliberately harming one. The issue arises when we purchase animal meat, as someone intentionally takes the animal's life on our behalf for consumption, unlike the accidental impacts in crop production.

Adopting a vegan lifestyle directly eliminates this cognitive dissonance, aligning our behaviour with our morals. Yet, humans resist behavioural changes that challenge their identity and cultural norms, often revealing conditioned responses rather than true principles.

Remarkably, industries have devised a system shielding consumers from the grim realities, outsourcing the dirty work to marginalised individuals. This allows consumers to enjoy their food without confronting cognitive dissonance directly.

However, if ethical reasons deter us from wielding the knife ourselves, can we morally justify having someone else do it on our behalf? And if we'd be willing to perform the act, can we ethically justify taking a life when it's unnecessary?

Our brain often employs creative strategies to mitigate cognitive dissonance. One common approach is viewing animals as objects or commodities. Yet, deep down, we acknowledge their distinct personalities, akin to our pets.

Another tactic involves belittling animals, convincing ourselves they can't truly feel pain or lack intelligence, although we know we cannot morally justify taking a life based on intellectual abilities.

However, our perspective changes when it comes to other animals, like pets or wild ones, recognising their sentience and right to live. Yet, there's a double standard in how we treat certain animals, a phenomenon termed 'speciesism'. While most people reject poaching and trophy hunting for causing unnecessary harm to animals, a similar act in a slaughterhouse is often accepted, reflecting the inherent bias in our treatment of different species.

What exactly is speciesism?

While racism, sexism, or speciesism are complex and different in many ways, these forms of oppression are rooted in the same hierarchical mindset: the idea that certain groups of individuals are superior to others because of arbitrary criteria such as race, gender, or species, which is the root cause of some of the biggest crimes against Humanity, especially the crimes against Black people throughout history such as slavery, colonisation, and neocolonisation. While the motives are different, the justifications used back then remain the same ones we currently use today to justify unnecessarily owning, exploiting, and killing farmed animals: "They are bred for that purpose", "They were put here for us", "God said it's ok", "They are different", "We are more intelligent", "We are superior".

It's easy to overlook, but amidst our differences from various species, it's crucial to remember that we are one of them – Homo sapiens. In simpler terms, we, too, are animals.

While it's widely accepted as morally wrong to commodify humans, the question arises: why would it be morally acceptable to commodify non-human animals?

This is the essence of speciesism: the belief that we have the right to choose which species are to be protected and which ones are to be exploited or killed for profit, simply because they are not human.

Whether discussing white supremacy, male supremacy, or human supremacy, we are essentially addressing the fight against the systemic oppression of a group denied the right to live and be free through political, economic, and institutional means. In simple terms, it's a struggle against the idea that one race, gender, or species should have the right to dominate, control, exploit, humiliate, abuse, or kill another with impunity.

All forms of oppression are interconnected, and justice must be blind to race, gender, and species to be morally consistent. It's a contradiction to claim to be against oppression while selectively supporting it. As Black liberation activist *Dick Gregory*, who embraced veganism in the 60s following *Martin Luther King*'s non-violence principles, aptly put it, "because I am a civil rights activist, I am also an animal rights activist. Animals and humans suffer and die alike. Violence causes the same pain, the same spilling of blood, the same stench of death, the same arrogant, cruel, and vicious taking of life. We shouldn't be a part of it".

Noteworthy figures such as *Coretta King* (Martin Luther King's widow), *Gandhi*, *Rosa Parks*, *Angela Davis*, and *Alice Walker* also abstained from consuming animal flesh for similar reasons, just like many non-Western cultures too, including Buddhists, Hindus, Rastafari, and other African cultures. As previously mentioned, avoiding unnecessary harm to non-human animals is not a Western trend; it is rooted in ancient moral philosophies across the world.

What about African communities that rely on the consumption of animals?

While we believe that the consumption of animals is justified in cases of necessity, particularly in specific rural areas, it's crucial to note that most of us, especially in African cities and in the West, do not depend on animal products for survival; rather, our consumption is driven by personal preference. Pleasure, notably the taste of meat, milk, and eggs, stands out as a primary motivator since we would never eat these products if we didn't like the way they taste. However, the ethical question arises – can any action be morally justified solely for pleasure, especially when it involves the exploitation, harm, commodification, or killing of someone?

While we all know the answer to this question, the challenge rather lies in how farmed animals have been marginalised to such a degree that they are not even recognised as victims, simply because they aren't humans or iconic species like elephants, giraffes, or lions. We believe that it's imperative to draw lessons from history and remember that normality does not equate to morality.

To achieve moral consistency, we believe justice must be blind to race, gender, and species. As Afro-feminist and social justice activist Alice Walker aptly stated, "*Animals were not made for humans, any more than black people were made for whites, or women for men*".

As previously stated, our intention is not about passing judgement; instead, it is an invitation to embrace more conscious choices that resonate with our souls.

How Does the Concept of Pan-Africanism Connect with These Ideas?

Transitioning to a plant-based food system holds numerous benefits for the continent. However, a crucial issue to tackle is neocolonisation. A more subtle yet equally oppressive force compared to colonisation, neocolonisation utilises indirect political, military, financial, economic, and cultural pressures to dominate, control, influence, and exploit other countries, particularly 'former' colonies.

Rooted in the commodification of people, animals, and nature, neocolonisation emerged in the 1960s as a replacement for direct colonisation. It enables the Western oligarchy to amass unlimited wealth by utilising free or cheap labour from the Global South to extract strategic resources needed by Western nations, often neglecting local communities and the environment. This imperialistic approach exacerbates the climate crisis and fuels ongoing conflicts around the globe.

Pan-Africanist leaders like *Ruben Um Nyobe* in Cameroon, *Kwame Nkrumah* in Ghana, *Patrice Lumumba* in DR Congo, or *Thomas Sankara* in Burkina Faso, who fought for the liberation of Africa, fell victim to this system. These African heroes envisioned a united and liberated continent, free from external manipulation and exploitation, prioritising self-determination, moral integrity, and unity among African nations. *Thomas Sankara*, in particular, demonstrated a strong commitment to public health, women rights, environmental and ecological issues, advocating for sustainability, local production, and consumption.

> "*Let's live as Africans, let's produce what we need, and consume what we produce.*"
>
> —*Thomas Sankara*

Unfortunately, these heroes ended up persecuted, imprisoned, and eventually killed by the West via coup d'état, either directly through Western forces or indirectly through corrupt African leaders, prioritising Western interests over their citizens'. This fuels further conflicts and hinders meaningful economic development in the region.

This historical perspective aligns with today's challenges of neocolonialism and environmental degradation across the continent. The cocoa production in both Ivory Coast and Ghana is a poignant example. These two countries produce about 70% of the global cocoa production, yet face issues like deforestation, child labour, modern slavery, and low farmer incomes, primarily due to Western corporations controlling prices. While these nations have enough land to feed their population, most of their soil is now dedicated to growing cocoa beans exported to Western nations for chocolate production, while relying on humanitarian aid to feed its citizens in need. Like a poisoned gift, these aids ingrains in our minds the illusion that Africa depends on the West when it is the opposite, since Africa has the richest soil on the planet. As Thomas Sankara once said: "*He who feeds you controls you.*"

Despite being plant-based, a food system based on this neocolonial capitalist structure would not be sustainable for the global African community, in Africa and beyond. To overcome neocolonisation, we need Pan-Africanism. African nations and the diaspora must unite, reclaim control of our resources, transform them locally, develop our own currencies, consume locally, export finished products, and ensure the benefits reach African people and the diaspora first, but for this, we need moral integrity (Maat). The vision is for a united Africa – a United States of Africa? This would benefit not only Africa but also the entire diaspora.

While acknowledging the causes, we believe it is essential to avoid a 'victim' mindset and instead focus on decolonising our mind, healing past traumas, empowering our community, and embracing our Africanity.

> *"I am not African because I was born in Africa, but because Africa was born in me."*
>
> *—Kwame Nkrumah*

Key Takeaways: What We Aim for You to Grasp from This?

Imagine a table set with delicious dishes that transcend geographical boundaries, rooted in the essence of our shared history and the resilience of our people. As we explore the richness of African cuisine with a plant-based twist, let each flavour serve as a reminder that, despite our diversity, we are connected by the same ancestral soil.

With its emphasis on ethics, justice, and integrity, veganism resonates deeply with the principles of Pan-Africanism, Maat, and Ubuntu. *Choosing a vegan lifestyle is not a restriction, but a liberation. It breaks free from this social conditioning, empowering us to make conscious choices in harmony with our principles – an act that not only nourishes our bodies but elevates our souls.*

More than a diet, a plant-based lifestyle is a gateway to a world of new flavours and unlimited culinary adventures, fostering a deeper connection to nature, our roots, and cultures.

In the spirit of Pan-Africanism, guided by Maat principles, Ubuntu wisdom, and the ethics of veganism, let these aunties-approved recipes, paired with our carefully selected playlists, be a vibrant culinary bridge that unites us all – from the richness of our soil to the depth of our soul.

Hotep!

SOUTHERN AFRICA RECIPES

A brief history of plant-based food in Southern Africa

Delving into Southern Africa's culinary narrative unveils a rich tapestry woven with historical roots and vibrant diversity. Traditional diets, anchored by staple grains like maize, millet, and sorghum, give rise to iconic dishes such as sadza, complemented by an array of vegetables and legumes. The inclusion of indigenous leafy greens, or 'morogo', and exotic fruits like marula and baobab adds a unique flair to the region's gastronomic tradition.

Embracing its cultural evolution, Southern African cuisine proudly features celebrated classics like 'samp and beans', a testament to indigenous South Africans. In the contemporary era, a renaissance in plant-based eating emerges, driven by a fusion of health consciousness and a rekindled appreciation for traditional fare. This culinary revival blends the heritage of Southern Africa with a modern perspective, offering a vibrant palette of plant-based dishes that vividly showcase the region's cultural richness and the bounty of its natural resources.

Scan for Immaculate Southern African Vibes

STREET FOOD SIDES SNACKS

South African Vetkoek and Curried Mince

Explore the delicious fusion of golden-fried dough pockets and a fragrantly spiced plant-based mince filling. This delightful pairing offers a symphony of textures and flavours from the south of the continent.

Prep Time: 30 minutes
Cook Time: 40 minutes
Total Time: 1 hour 10 minutes
Difficulty: Intermediate

Ingredients (serves 6–8)

For Vetkoek:

- 800 g all-purpose flour
- 1 tbsp sugar
- 1 tsp salt
- 1 tbsp instant yeast
- 250 ml warm water
- Vegetable oil for frying

For Curried Mince:

- 800g plant-based mince (e.g. soy mince)
- 1 onion, finely chopped
- 2 garlic cloves, minced
- 2 tbsp curry powder
- 4 tomatoes, diced
- 250 ml vegetable broth
- Salt and pepper to taste

Note: If soy mince is not available, we recommend baked tofu crumbles, finely chopped mushrooms, or black beans.

How to Prepare

Prepare Vetkoek:

- Add the warm water, yeast, and sugar in a bowl. Mix and let sit for 5 minutes. Then add the flour and salt to form a soft dough. Knead for 5–7 minutes, then cover with a clean cloth.
- Allow the dough to rest for at least 1 hour or until it has doubled in size.
- Pinch off a piece of dough about the size of a tennis ball and on a clean surface, roll until smooth. Then flatten the ball until it is palm-sized and set aside on a floured work surface. Repeat with the remaining dough.
- Heat vegetable oil in a pot. Drop the dough balls into the hot oil and fry until golden brown on both sides. Then place to drain on paper towels.

Make the Curried Mince:

- Sauté chopped onions and garlic until softened in a pan.
- Add plant-based mince and curry powder. Cook until browned.
- Stir in diced tomatoes and vegetable broth. Simmer until the mixture thickens.
- Season with salt and pepper.
- Enjoy with the Vetkoek.

Storage and Leftovers

Refrigeration: *Store Vetkoek and curried mince separately in airtight containers in the refrigerator for up to 3–4 days.*

Chamuças Moçambicanas

These flaky pastry pockets embrace a rich filling of spiced goodness. Crafted with the vibrant flavours of Mozambique, these savoury treats offer a delightful blend of aromas that celebrate the region's culinary heritage.

Prep Time: 40 minutes
Cook Time: 20 minutes
Total Time: 1 hour
Difficulty: Intermediate

Ingredients (serves 4–6)

- 400 g lentils, cooked and mashed
- 2 carrots, grated
- 2 onions, finely chopped
- 2 garlic cloves, minced
- 1 tsp ground cumin
- 1 tsp ground coriander
- 1 tsp curry powder
- Spring roll or samosa dough sheets (store-bought or self-made)
- Vegetable oil for frying

How to Prepare

- In a pan, sauté chopped onions and garlic until softened.
- Add grated carrots, mashed lentils, ground cumin, coriander, and curry powder. Cook until well combined.
- Allow the mixture to cool.
- Place a spoonful of the lentil mixture onto a spring roll wrapper and fold according to package instructions.
- Fry the chamuças until golden brown.

Storage and Leftovers

Refrigeration: *Store in an airtight container in the refrigerator for up to 3–4 days.*

HEARTY MAIN DISHES

Mozambican Piri Piri Cauliflower Steaks

Tender cauliflower slices are infused with the fiery kick of Piri Piri spices. These steaks offer a delightful combination of smokiness and heat, showcasing Mozambique's bold and vibrant flavours.

Prep Time: 20 minutes
Marination Time: 1 hour
Cook Time: 30 minutes
Total Time: 1 hour 50 minutes
Difficulty: Intermediate

Ingredients (serves 4)

For Cauliflower Steaks:

- 1 large cauliflower head, leaves removed

For Piri Piri Marinade:

- 4 red African bird-eyes chillies
- 2 red bell pepper, chopped
- 1 red onion, chopped
- 4 garlic cloves
- 2 tbsp lemon juice
- 1 tsp dried oregano
- 1 tsp black pepper
- 1 tsp salt
- 1 tsp smoked paprika
- 4 tbsp vegetable oil

How to Prepare

Prepare Piri Piri Marinade:

- Blend all the ingredients until smooth. Set aside.

Prepare the Cauliflower:

- Trim the cauliflower stem, leaving the head intact.
- Slice the cauliflower into thick steaks, about 1–1.5 inches wide.
- Spread the Piri Piri marinade on both sides of the cauliflower and let it marinate for 1 hour.
- Then preheat the oven to 200°C (400°F).
- Place the marinated cauliflower steaks on a baking sheet lined with parchment paper.
- Roast in the oven for 25–30 minutes or until the cauliflower is tender and golden brown. Turn half way through cooking time to ensure they are well cooked.
- Garnish with additional chopped parsley, and serve the Piri Piri cauliflower steaks with your favourite sides.

Storage and Leftovers

Refrigeration: *Store any leftovers in an airtight container in the refrigerator for 2–3 days.*

Madagascan Ravitoto

This traditional dish combines cassava leaves with coconut, creating a rich and hearty stew.

Prep Time: 30 minutes
Cook Time: 1 hour
Total Time: 1 hour 30 minutes
Difficulty: Intermediate

Ingredients (serves 4)

For Ravitoto:

- 500 g cassava leaves, chopped
- 300 g spinach, chopped
- 250 ml coconut milk
- 4 tomatoes, diced
- 1 onion, finely chopped
- 2 garlic cloves, minced
- 2 tbsp vegetable oil
- 2 tsp ground ginger
- Salt and pepper to taste

For Rice:

- 500 g white rice, cooked

For Rougail:

- 2 tomatoes, diced
- 1 onion, finely chopped
- 1 handful fresh coriander, chopped

For Spicy Sauce:

- 2 tbsp vegetable oil
- 1 onion, finely chopped
- 2 garlic cloves, minced
- 1 tbsp ground ginger
- 1 tsp cayenne pepper
- 1 scotch bonnet (depending on spice preference)
- Salt to taste

How to Prepare

Prepare Ravitoto:

- Sauté chopped onions and garlic in vegetable oil until softened in a pot.
- Add cassava leaves, spinach, coconut milk, diced tomatoes, salt, and pepper. Cook until the leaves are tender.

Prepare Rice:

- Cook white rice according to package instructions.

Prepare Rougail:

- Mix diced tomatoes, chopped onions, and fresh coriander in a bowl.

Prepare Spicy Sauce:

- Sauté chopped onions and garlic in vegetable oil in a saucepan until softened.
- Add ginger, ground cayenne pepper, scotch bonnet, and salt. Cook until fragrant.
- Plate everything as desired (some mix everything, others keep it separate) and serve.

Storage and Leftovers

Refrigeration: *Store Ravitoto, rice, rougail, and spicy sauce separately in airtight containers in the refrigerator for up to 3–4 days.*

DELICIOUS DESSERTS

South African Malva Pudding

This beloved dessert is a perfect blend of rich toffee and apricot jam (or a jam of your choice). It is served warm with a drizzle of velvety caramel sauce, encapsulating the heart-warming essence of South African hospitality and culinary delight.

Prep Time: 20 minutes
Cook Time: 30 minutes
Total Time: 50 minutes
Difficulty: Easy

Ingredients (serves 4)

For Pudding:

- 120 g all-purpose flour
- 250 ml plant-based milk
- 200 g sugar
- 2 tbsp apricot jam (or jam of your choice)
- 1 tbsp white vinegar
- 1 tsp baking soda
- Pinch of salt
- 2 tbsp plant-based butter, melted

For Sauce:

- 250 ml plant-based cream
- 120 g plant-based butter
- 100 g sugar
- 1 tsp vanilla extract

How to Prepare

Prepare Pudding:

- Preheat the oven to 180°C (350°F) and grease a baking dish.
- Mix flour, plant-based milk, sugar, apricot jam, vinegar, baking soda, salt, and melted vegan butter in a bowl until well combined.
- Pour the batter into the prepared baking dish.
- Bake for 30 minutes or until the pudding is golden brown and set.

Prepare Sauce:

- Heat plant-based cream, vegan butter, sugar, and vanilla extract in a saucepan until the sugar is dissolved.
- Pour the warm sauce over the baked pudding and let it soak in before serving.

Storage and Leftovers

Refrigeration: *Store any leftovers in an airtight container in the refrigerator for 3–4 days.*

Mozambican Coconut Cake

Delight in the tropical bliss of Mozambican Coconut Cake, a beloved dessert that transports you to sun-kissed shores. This luscious cake, infused with the rich essence of coconut, offers a taste of paradise.

Prep Time: 15 minutes
Cook Time: 40 minutes
Total Time: 55 minutes
Difficulty: Easy

Ingredients (serves 8)

- 240 g all-purpose flour
- 200 g sugar
- 80 g desiccated coconut
- 250 ml plant-based milk
- 100 ml vegetable oil
- 2 tsp baking powder
- 1 tsp vanilla extract
- Zest of 1 lime (optional)

How to Prepare

- Preheat the oven to 180°C (350°F) and grease a cake pan.
- Mix dry ingredients in a bowl – flour, sugar, coconut, and baking powder.
- Add plant-based milk, vegetable oil, vanilla extract, and lime zest (if using). Mix until just combined.
- Pour the batter into the prepared cake pan and bake for 40 minutes or until a knife inserted comes out clean.

Storage and Leftovers

Room Temperature: *Store in an airtight container at room temperature for up to 2 days.*

EASTERN AFRICA RECIPES

A brief history of plant-based food in East Africa

Embark on a culinary journey through East Africa, where the roots of plant-based eating run deep. Traditional diets, adorned with staples like sorghum, millet, teff, leafy greens, legumes, and root vegetables, vividly depict a region steeped in wholesome, plant-centric nutrition. Imagine the delightful aroma of Injera, a fermented teff flatbread, gracing the tables of Eritrea and Ethiopia, symbolising the rich heritage of plant-based indulgence.

The diverse geography of East Africa gifts the region with an array of indigenous fruits and vegetables, infusing local cuisines with unique flavours. Along the Swahili coast, coastal areas elevate their plant-based culinary traditions with coconut-based curries and spiced rice, creating a symphony of tastes that captivate the senses.

In the contemporary era, East Africa continues to embrace the essence of plant-based living, motivated by a harmonious blend of health and environmental consciousness. The region's culinary tapestry weaves traditional and modern plant-based dishes, responding to the evolving global palate with a fusion of culturally rich cuisine and sustainable nutrition. Join the celebration of East Africa's plant-powered legacy, where each dish tells a story of tradition, health, and a vibrant culinary future.

Scan for Authentic East African Rhythms

STREET FOOD
SIDES
SNACKS

Dabo Kolo

This delightful snack is in Ethiopian and Congolese cuisine. Indulge in the crunchy, bite-sized pieces, each seasoned with a blend of spices, offering a taste of tradition and a crispy adventure for your taste buds.

Prep Time: 15 minutes
Cook Time: 30 minutes
Total Time: 45 minutes
Difficulty: Intermediate

Ingredients (serves 4)

- 240 g all-purpose flour
- ½ tsp salt
- 1 tbsp sugar
- 1 tbsp cayenne pepper or cinnamon (if you want it sweet or savoury)
- 60 ml vegetable oil
- 125 ml water

How to Prepare

- Combine all-purpose flour, sugar, baking powder, ground cayenne pepper or cinnamon, and salt in a bowl.
- Pour vegetable oil and mix with hands.
- Pour the water into the dough, little by little, kneading in between. The dough should not be sticky or crumbly. Once all the water has been added, use your hands to knead for 5 minutes.
- Flour a dry, flat surface and roll the dough out with a rolling pin until it's about ¼ inch thick. Then, cut the dough into strips lengthwise and horizontally. The pieces should be about ½ inch on all sides (except for thickness).
- Heat a non-stick pan over medium heat with no oil or grease. Add the pieces (gently) to the pan and mix occasionally for about 20 minutes until they're toasted on all sides.
- Alternatively, you could bake them in the oven at 200°C for 25–30 minutes or until golden brown.
- Allow them to cool before serving.

Storage and Leftovers

Room Temperature: *Store in an airtight container at room temperature for up to 1 week.*

Kenyan Kachumbari

This is a refreshing salad bursting with tomatoes, onions, coriander, and chilli. This zesty dish offers a harmonious blend of fresh ingredients that will brighten any meal.

Prep Time: 15 minutes
Cook Time: 0 minutes
Total Time: 15 minutes
Difficulty: Easy

Ingredients (serves 4)

- 4 tomatoes, sliced
- 1 red onion, sliced
- 1 cucumber, sliced
- 2 green chillies, finely chopped
- 1 bunch coriander, chopped
- Juice of 2 limes
- Salt and pepper to taste

How to Prepare

- Combine diced tomatoes, finely chopped red onion, diced cucumber, finely chopped green chillies, and chopped coriander in a large bowl.
- Squeeze the juice of 2 limes over the mixture.
- Season with salt and pepper to taste.
- Toss the ingredients until well combined.
- Refrigerate for at least 30 minutes before serving.

Storage and Leftovers

Refrigeration: *Kachumbari can be stored in the refrigerator for 2 days. Ensure it's in an airtight container.*

Mini Mandazi

These deep-fried dough balls are an East African street food delicacy that perfectly balances the sweetness of coconut milk with a hint of spice.

Prep Time: 20 minutes
Cook Time: 20 minutes
Total Time: 40 minutes
Difficulty: Intermediate

Ingredients (serves 4)

- 400 g self-raising flour, plus 10 g for kneading
- 50 g sugar
- 250 ml coconut milk
- 60 g plant-based butter, melted
- ¼ tsp ground cinnamon or cardamom (optional)
- Vegetable oil for frying

How to Prepare

- Combine flour, sugar, and ground cinnamon or cardamom (if using) in a bowl. Add coconut milk and melted butter.
- Knead the mixture into a soft dough for about 5–10 minutes. Add extra flour if it is too wet and sticky.
- Rest for 10 minutes. Divide in 2 and roll out to about an inch of thickness on a floured surface.
- Cut into diamonds.
- Heat vegetable oil in a pan and fry the Mandazi until golden brown on both sides.
- Avoid using high heat when cooking Mandazi as this will make them hard on the outside and undercooked on the inside. Use medium heat.
- Remove from the oil and drain on paper towels.
- Enjoy with tea or coffee!

Storage and Leftovers

Room Temperature: *Mandazi can be stored at room temperature for up to 2 days in an airtight container.*

Ugandan Rolex

Rolex isn't just a watch; it's also this very popular timeless "Rolled Eggs" street food wrapped up in a chapati. Traditionally made of eggs, we recommend this mind-blowing omelette recipe with a plant-based twist. This savoury delight is a taste of Uganda's culinary creativity, offering a fusion of textures and flavours in every bite.

Prep Time: 15 minutes
Cook Time: 10 minutes
Total Time: 25 minutes
Difficulty: Easy

Ingredients (serves 2)

For Chapatis:

- 2 chapatis (store-bought or homemade)

For Plant-Based Omelette:

- 60 g chickpea flour
- 125 ml soy milk for neutral flavour (or any other plant-based milk)
- 1 tbsp nutrition yeast
- 1 tbsp Kala Namak black salt (for egg flavour)
- 1 tsp white pepper
- 1 tsp garlic powder
- Vegetable oil

For Omelette Filling:

- 4 large tomatoes, sliced
- 1 red onion, thinly sliced
- ¼ white cabbage, thinly sliced

How to Prepare

Prepare Plant-Based Omelette:

- Blend chickpea flour, plant-based milk, nutrition yeast, black salt, white pepper, and garlic powder. The texture should be thicker than a crepe but thinner than a pancake.
- Grease a frying pan with oil.
- Once hot, add the mixture and cook on medium heat.
- Once nearly dry on top, flip it.

Prepare Rolex:

- Place the chapati on top of the omelette and carefully flip it so the chapati warms up.
- Place on a plate, add tomatoes, cabbage, and onion.
- Roll the chapati to form the Rolex and enjoy!

Storage and Leftovers

Refrigeration: *Rolex is best enjoyed fresh, but if you have leftovers, refrigerate in an airtight containers.*

Injera

This is the star of any East African dish. It's a tangy soft bread that captures the essence of the cuisine in the Horn of Africa.

Prep Time: 3 days
Cook Time: 1 hour
Total Time: 3 days and 1 hour
Difficulty: Intermediate

Ingredients (serves 6)

- 2 kg teff flour
- 1 tsp active dry yeast
- 1.5 L water for step 1 (starter)
- 715 ml water for step 2 (absit)
- Vegetable oil

How to Prepare

Step 1: Starter

- In a bucket or large bowl, mix dry yeast and some water.
- Add teff flour then gradually add water. Knead well by hand. Ensure the mixture is sticky, then cover it with a layer of water.
- Close the bucket and let it ferment for 4 days (about 3 days in summer/about 4–5 days in winter).

Step 2: Absit

- After 4 days, gently drain the upper liquid. Mix well by hand.
- Boil about 475 ml of water in a small pot. In the meantime, mix one ladle of the dough with one ladle of water from the pot in another bowl to dilute the dough.
- Stir well. This will prevent lumps.
- Add the diluted mixture into the pot once the water boils while stirring continuously until it becomes thicker.
- Let it sit for about 20 minutes and stir occasionally so the bottom does not stick.
- After 20 minutes, let the mixture cool down until lukewarm. Once lukewarm, add the mixture into the bucket. Mix very well with the dough.
- Add about 120 ml of water and mix well until the water is absorbed.
- Keep mixing and add another 120 ml of water to cover the mixture with a bit of water. Close the bucket and let it sit overnight (6–12 hours in summer/24 hours in winter).

Step 3: Cooking

- Drain the upper liquid. Mix well by hand until very smooth. The mixture should be thicker than a crepe but thinner than a pancake.
- Grease a non-sticky pan with some oil, then pour the mixture and let it cook.
- Once about 80% of the injera is covered with small holes, cover the pan for about 30–40 seconds. Do not flip the injera.
- Remove the Injera and repeat the process with the remaining batter.
- Serve the injera with your favourite East African plant-based stews or dips and enjoy!

Storage and Leftovers

Refrigeration: *Store Injera and stews separately in airtight containers. They can be refrigerated for up to 3–4 days.*
Freezing: *Injera is best enjoyed fresh.*

HEARTY MAIN DISHES

Kik Alicha

Savour the diverse flavours of delicate and creamy Kik Alicha, an East African Yellow Split Pea Stew. Enjoy with tangy Injera for an authentic East African experience!

Prep Time: 30 minutes
Cook Time: 1 hour
Total Time: 1 hour 30 minutes
Difficulty: Intermediate

Ingredients (serves 4)

- 250 g yellow split peas
- 2 onions, finely chopped
- 5 garlic cloves, minced
- 2 tbsp berbere spice mix (see Herbs and Spices section for exact spices)
- 235 ml water
- Salt and pepper to taste
- Vegetable oil

How to Prepare

- In a pot, boil the split peas until slightly soft. Drain and set aside.
- Dice the onions and thinly slice the garlic.
- In the same pot, heat the cooking oil over medium heat.
- Add the diced onions and sliced garlic to the pot and sauté until they become fragrant and translucent.
- Stir in the berbere spice mix, ensuring the onions and garlic are well-coated.
- Add the cooked peas to the pot and mix them with the spiced onion and garlic mixture.
- Season with salt to taste and pour in the cup of water. Stir well.
- Place a lid on the pan and let the stew cook until the peas are soft.
- Serve on Injera bread or in a bowl.

Storage and Leftovers

Refrigeration: *Store stew in an airtight container. Kik Alicha can be refrigerated for up to 3–4 days.*
Freezing: *Kik Alicha can be frozen for up to 2–3 months. Thaw and reheat when ready to eat.*

Tanzanian Mchuzi wa Biringani

Discover this rich Tanzanian aubergine curry that offers a rich blend of spices and textures.

Prep Time: 20 minutes
Cook Time: 30 minutes
Total Time: 50 minutes
Difficulty: Intermediate

Ingredients (serves 4)

- 2 large aubergines, cubed
- 1 onion, finely chopped
- 2 garlic cloves, minced
- 1 can chopped tomatoes
- 1 tbsp curry powder
- 1 tsp ground turmeric
- 1 tsp ground cumin
- 1 tsp ground coriander
- ½ tsp cayenne pepper
- 250 ml coconut milk (optional)
- Vegetable oil
- Salt to taste

How to Prepare

- Sauté chopped onions and garlic in oil until softened.
- Add curry powder, turmeric, cumin, coriander, and cayenne. Cook for a minute ensuring onions and garlic are well covered.
- Add cubed aubergines, crushed tomatoes, and salt. Simmer until aubergines are tender.
- Add coconut milk for creaminess if desired.
- Serve with rice and/or bread.

Storage and Leftovers

Refrigeration: *Store in an airtight container in the refrigerator for up to 3–4 days.*
Freezing: *The curry can be frozen for 2–3 months. Thaw and reheat when ready to eat.*

Tanzanian Wali na Maharage

The national dish of Tanzania combines fragrant rice with aromatic beans creating a delightful harmony of flavour in every mouthful.

Prep Time: 15 minutes
Cook Time: 45 minutes
Total Time: 1 hour
Difficulty: Easy

Ingredients (serves 2)

- 1 kg white rice
- 1 can kidney beans, drained and rinsed
- 2 onions, finely chopped
- 2 garlic cloves, minced
- 1 carrot, chopped
- 1 can chopped tomatoes
- 250 ml coconut milk
- 1 tsp ground cumin
- 1 tsp paprika
- Vegetable oil
- Salt to taste

How to Prepare

- Rinse rice and cook according to package instructions.
- Sauté chopped onions, garlic, and carrot in oil until softened.
- Once softened, add ground cumin, and paprika and cook for another minute. Then add chopped tomatoes and stir well.
- Add drained kidney beans and salt. Cook until beans are heated through.
- Add coconut milk and stir. Reduce the heat to low and simmer for 5 minutes, stirring occasionally.
- Serve the beans over cooked rice.

Storage and Leftovers

Refrigeration: *Store rice and beans separately in airtight containers. They can be refrigerated for up to 3–4 days.*
Freezing: *Both rice and beans can be frozen for up to 2–3 months. Thaw and reheat when ready to eat.*

DELICIOUS DESSERTS

Tanzanian Vitumbua

Enjoy these golden, coconut-infused doughnuts – a delightful fusion of tradition and flavour that will transport you to the heart of Tanzanian culinary bliss.

Prep Time: 15 minutes
Cook Time: 30 minutes
Total Time: 45 minutes
Difficulty: Easy

Ingredients (serves 4)

- 310 g rice flour
- 120 ml coconut milk
- 50 g sugar
- 1 tsp baking powder
- ½ tsp ground cardamom
- Vegetable oil for frying

How to Prepare

- Mix rice flour, sugar, baking powder, and ground cardamom in a bowl. Slowly add the coconut milk to form a dough.
- Heat vegetable oil in an aebleskiver pan.
- Drop spoonfuls of the batter into the hot oil and fry until golden brown on both sides.
- Remove from the oil and drain on paper towels.

Storage and Leftovers

Room Temperature: *Store in an airtight container at room temperature for up to 2 days.*

Ugandan Sim-Sim Cookies

Indulge in these sesame-studded delights that encapsulate the essence of tradition and sweetness.

Prep Time: 20 minutes
Cook Time: 15 minutes
Cooling Time: 2 hours
Total Time: 2 hours 35 minutes
Difficulty: Intermediate

Ingredients (serves 4-6)

- 150 g sesame seeds
- 150 g sugar

How to Prepare

- In a pot, melt sugar on low heat until caramelised, stirring continuously.
- Add the sesame seeds to the melted sugar.
- Keep an eye on it constantly and stir it gently to bring it together.
- Be careful not to let the mixture cook too long, or the cookies will be too brittle.
- Pour the hot mixture onto a flat, greased surface. Work quickly to pat or roll the hot mixture into a flat, approximately ¼-inch-thick sheet.
- Cool until warm to the touch, but not hot and slice into squares.
- Separate the square cookies and remove them to another surface to continue cooling.

Storage and Leftovers

Room Temperature: *Store in an airtight container at room temperature for up to 1 week.*

CENTRAL AFRICA RECIPES

A brief history of plant-based food in Central Africa

Embark on a culinary journey through Central Africa, where the lush tropical rainforests and diverse cultures weave a captivating plant-based tradition. At the heart of this vibrant culinary heritage are staples like cassava, yams, plantains, and leafy greens, crafting exquisite dishes like Saka Saka or Ndole.

These delights are paired with flavourful vegetable-based sauces, featuring the richness of palm nuts and oil palm fruit, while tropical fruits like bananas and pineapples provide a sweet symphony of flavours. Immerse yourself in the enchanting fusion of flavours, a testament to the depth and allure of Central Africa's plant-based culinary artistry.

Scan for Flawless Central African Vibes

STREET FOOD SIDES SNACKS

Cameroonian Beignets Haricots Bouillie (BHB)

Savour the crispy perfection of these deep-fried dough delights, served with flavourful beans and corn porridge (locally called Paf) – a tantalising combination often nicknamed BHB. Beignets is another name for Puff Puff, Mikate, or Atchomo, essentially fried dough balls. In Cameroon, this very popular street food, naturally vegan, is usually eaten for breakfast, although some people can have it all day!

Prep Time: 20 minutes
Cook Time: 20 minutes
Total Time: 40 minutes
Difficulty: Easy

Ingredients (serves 4)

For the Beignets:

- 475 g warm water
- 12 g active dry yeast
- 140 g sugar
- 500 g all-purpose flour
- ½ tsp salt
- 1.5 L vegetable oil

For the Haricots:

- 250 g dry red beans, soaked overnight (or tinned black-eyed peas)
- 2 onions, chopped
- ½ tsp baking soda
- Vegetable oil
- 3 garlic cloves
- 3 tomatoes, chopped (or 1 tin chopped tomatoes)
- 1 tbsp ginger
- 100 g vegetable stock
- 1 bay leaf
- 1 sprig of fresh thyme
- 1 scotch bonnet (depending on spice preference)
- Salt and pepper to taste

How to Prepare

Prepare the Beignets:

- Dissolve the yeast in half of the water in a bowl.
- Dissolve the sugar in the remaining water in another bowl.
- Sift the flour and add the salt in a large bowl or pan.
- Mix in the sugar-water.
- Add the yeast-water and mix.
- Beat the dough vigorously until smooth.
- Cover with a damp cloth or plastic wrap and let it rise for 2 hours in an oven or at room temperature if not too cold.
- Heat oil in a deep pot until hot. (Test the heat by dropping a tiny bit of dough; it should sizzle and come to the surface.)
- Wet your hands, scoop some dough, and drop a ball into the hot oil. Alternatively, use a spoon.
- Fry at medium heat until golden-brown.
- Remove and place on a paper towel to absorb the oil.

Prepare the Haricots:

- Soak the beans overnight or for 8 hours. (If using tinned beans, no need to soak.)
- Drain the water, rinse, and place the beans in a large pan covered in cold water.
- Add chopped onions, cover, and cook for 35 minutes until tender. Add the baking soda once it starts boiling.
- Mix the tomatoes, onions, ginger, and garlic in a blender.
- Heat the oil in a large pan.
- Add the tomato-onion mixture and cook on medium heat for 10 minutes, stirring occasionally to avoid burning.
- Add the water, salt, and pepper to taste. Cook for 5 minutes.
- Add the beans. Cook for 5 minutes.

© Jessica Sagou Wikimedia

For the Corn Porridge (Paf):
- 6 tsp cornstarch
- 500 ml of soy milk
- Lemongrass stalks (optional)
- Sugar to taste (optional)

- Add the thyme and bay leaf. Cover and cook for 5 minutes.
- Turn off the heat, add the scotch bonnet pepper, and cover.
- Serve with the beignets and enjoy as a starter or side!

Prepare the Corn Porridge (Paf):
- Combine the cornstarch with a small amount of soy milk in a mixing bowl. Mix well to dissolve the cornstarch and create a smooth paste. Set aside.
- In a saucepan, heat the remaining soy milk over medium heat. Add lemongrass stalks to infuse flavour (optional). Allow the soy milk to come to a gentle simmer while stirring occasionally.
- Once the soy milk is simmering, gradually add the cornstarch paste to the saucepan while continuously stirring to avoid lumps.
- Keep stirring the mixture over medium heat until it thickens to your desired consistency. Adjust the thickness by adding more cornstarch or soy milk if needed.
- If you prefer a sweet porridge, add sugar to taste. Stir until the sugar is fully dissolved.
- Continue to cook the porridge for an additional 5–7 minutes, ensuring it reaches a smooth and creamy texture.
- Remove the lemongrass stalks before serving and pour the corn porridge into serving bowls.
- Dip your beignets in the Paf and enjoy!

Storage and Leftovers

Beignet-Haricot: *Store in an airtight container at room temperature for up to 2 days.*

Corn Porridge: *Cool andR store leftover corn in an airtight container in the fridge for 2–3 days. Reheating: Heat the desired amount in a saucepan, stir in soy milk if needed, and serve once heated through.*

Central and West African Soya

Experience the unique flavours of classic Central and West African street food with our perfectly charred oyster mushrooms soya. A plant-based take on the king of street food in the region.

Prep Time: 15 minutes
Cook Time: 10–15 minutes
Total Time: 25–30 minutes
Difficulty: Easy

Ingredients (serves 4)

- 300 g of oyster mushrooms (cooked jackfruit if not available)
- ½ tsp salt
- 2 tsp black pepper
- 2 tsp all-purpose seasoning
- 100 g soya pepper
- 2 tbsp vegetable oil
- 1 tomato, chopped
- 1 white onion, sliced
- If there is no soya pepper, blend roasted peanuts with garlic powder, onion powder, smoked paprika, ground ginger, cayenne pepper, and all-purpose seasoning.

How to Prepare

- Remove any excess moisture from your washed mushrooms by squeezing them.
- Shred to create more pieces.
- Mix mushrooms with salt, black pepper, all-purpose seasoning, and soya pepper in a bowl. Make sure to cover all sides.
- Heat 2 tbsp of oil in a cast-iron skillet, a grilled pan, or a frying pan (medium-high heat).
- Fry mushrooms in batch on both sides until char. 5–10 minutes.
- Repeat with the remaining mushrooms.
- Serve on an old newspaper or kraft brown paper. Cover mushrooms with additional soya pepper if needed.
- Sprinkle raw onion slices and chopped tomatoes. Grab a toothpick and enjoy!

Storage and Leftovers

Refrigeration: *Store leftovers in an airtight container in the refrigerator for up to 2–3 days.*

Congolese Fried Cassava

Why not savour the crispy goodness of fried cassava, a simple yet delicious culinary stable? Tasty as a side dish or snack!

Prep Time: 20 minutes
Cook Time: 20 minutes
Total Time: 40 minutes
Difficulty: Easy

Ingredients (serves 4)

- 500 g cassava, peeled and cut into large chunks
- Vegetable oil for frying
- Smoked paprika and salt to taste

How to Prepare

- Boil the cassava chunks until fork tender (about 20 minutes).
- Slice the cassava into sticks.
- Heat vegetable oil in a deep pan for frying.
- Fry cassava sticks until golden brown and crispy.
- Remove from the oil and drain on paper towels.
- Season with smoked paprika and salt to taste.

Storage and Leftovers

Room Temperature: *Store in an airtight container at room temperature for up to 2 days.*

HEARTY MAIN DISHES

Cameroonian Ndole with Fried Plantains

Welcome to the heart of Douala in Cameroon! In 2023, this royal dish from "Le Continent" was listed in the top 50 best traditional stews in the world by TasteAtlas. Traditionally served with Miondo (mashed cassava steamed into strips), this national treasure made from indigenous bitterleaves and peanut paste takes a simple twist with fried plantains and rice.

Prep Time: 30 minutes
Cook Time: 1 hour
Total Time: 1 hour 30 minutes
Difficulty: Intermediate

Ingredients (serves 4-6)

For Ndole:

- 500 g bitterleaves, finely chopped and washed (substitute with spinach if unavailable)
- 300 g blanched peanuts
- 1 large onion, sliced
- 4 garlic cloves, minced
- 1 thumb of ginger, grated
- Vegetable oil
- 2 scotch bonnets
- 2 tbsp all-purpose seasoning
- 240 ml vegetable broth
- 2 tbsp homemade nori powder (dried mushrooms and nori sheets ground together for a crayfish alternative)
- Salt and pepper to taste
- Optional meat alternative: tempeh or canned jackfruit chunks (be aware fresh takes longer to cook)

For Fried Plantains:

- 4 ripe plantains, peeled and sliced
- Approx. 240 ml vegetable oil

How to Prepare

Prepare Ndole:

- Boil the peanuts in a saucepan for about 15–20 minutes. There should be just enough water to cover the peanuts.
- Boil the bitterleaves for 10 minutes. Drain and rinse thoroughly. Repeat 2 additional times to remove bitterness.
- Blend the peanuts and scotch bonnets in a food processor, using the remaining water to facilitate the blending. Blend until you have a slightly grainy paste.
- Sauté sliced onions and garlic in vegetable oil in a pot.
- Add the peanut paste and ginger, and season with salt, pepper, and all-purpose seasoning.
- Add the broth and stir well. If you use tempeh or jackfruit chunks as a meat alternative, add them here.
- Let simmer for about 20–30 minutes.
- Add nori powder (optional crayfish alternative), the washed bitterleaves and salt and pepper to taste. Drizzle with oil and let simmer for about 10–15 minutes.

Prepare Plantains:

- Heat vegetable oil over medium-high heat in a separate pan.
- Fry plantain slices until golden brown on each side. Remove and place on a paper towel to absorb excess oil. Serve with Ndole and rice. Enjoy!

Storage and Leftovers

Refrigeration: *Store Ndole and the fried plantains separately in airtight containers in the refrigerator for up to 3–4 days.*

Congolese Saka Saka

Welcome to DR Congo! Indulge in the rich flavours of Saka Saka (cassava leaves), also known as Pondu in Congo, a traditional Congolese dish. Usually cooked with fish, we are purposely not suggesting any alternatives as we like it the way it is. Delight in the fusion of cassava leaves, peanuts, and aromatic spices, served alongside rice or plantains for a wholesome meal.

Prep Time: 15 minutes
Cook Time: 2 hours 45 minutes
Total Time: 3 hours
Difficulty: Moderate

Ingredients (serves 4-6)

- 500 g of cassava leaves, defrosted, and drained
- 1 scotch bonnet
- 1 aubergine
- 3 green bell peppers
- 1 stalk of celery
- 2 onions
- 7 garlic cloves
- 5 tbsp peanut butter, melted
- 1 tbsp palm oil (or vegetable oil)
- 1 L water
- 1 tsp sea salt
- 1 tsp black pepper
- 1 tbsp all-purpose seasoning

How to Prepare

- Mix onions, garlic, aubergine, celery, and bell peppers in a blender. Set aside.
- Add the Saka Saka leaves in a large pot on medium heat and stir for 2–3 minutes.
- Add the above-blended vegetables with 1 L of water. Stir.
- Bring the mixture to a boil, then reduce the heat and cook it for 30 minutes. Stir occasionally.
- Add palm oil, all-purpose seasoning, and a pinch of salt. Let it cook for 2 hours. Stir occasionally.
- Add peanut butter and scotch bonnet, and stir. Let it simmer for 15 minutes, stirring occasionally.
- Serve with rice or plantains and enjoy!

Storage and Leftovers

Refrigeration: *Store the cooked Saka Saka in airtight containers. It can be refrigerated for up to 3–4 days. Ensure the stew is properly cooled before transferring it to the refrigerator to maintain its freshness and prevent spoilage.*

DELICIOUS DESSERTS

Sweet Potato Cake

Velvety sweet potatoes are transformed into a moist and flavourful treat. Crafted with care, this cake is a harmonious blend of cinnamon, nutmeg, and a hint of vanilla, creating the perfect soul food.

Prep Time: 20 minutes
Cook Time: 30 minutes
Total Time: 50 minutes
Difficulty: Intermediate

Ingredients (serves 8-10)

- 1 kg sweet potatoes, boiled and mashed
- 310 g coconut milk
- 375 g all-purpose flour
- 160 g brown sugar or coconut sugar
- 125 g vegetable oil
- 3 tsp baking powder
- ½ tsp baking soda
- 1 tsp cinnamon
- 1 tsp nutmeg
- Pinch of salt

How to Prepare

- Preheat the oven to 180°C (350°F). Grease or line a 9-inch (23 cm) or 8-inch (20 cm) square baking pan with parchment paper.
- Add all the wet ingredients to a large mixing bowl and mix until there are no lumps. Add all the dry ingredients to the bowl and mix until there are no pockets of flour or wet ingredients. Be careful not to overmix the batter!
- Pour the batter into your cake tin. Bake for 30 minutes or until you can insert a knife or toothpick in the middle and it comes out clean.
- Allow the cake to cool in the tin. Serve with your favourite plant-based icing with tea or coffee!

Storage and Leftovers

Refrigeration: *Store in an airtight container in the refrigerator for up to 3–4 days.*

Central African Republic Banana Fritters

Infused with the warmth of cinnamon, the richness of nutmeg, and a touch of vanilla, these fritters are a delectable showcase of Central African sweetness.

Prep Time: 15 minutes
Cook Time: 15 minutes
Total Time: 30 minutes
Difficulty: Easy

Ingredients (serves 6-8)

- 4 ripe bananas, mashed
- 120 g all-purpose flour
- 50 g sugar
- 1 tsp baking powder
- ½ tsp ground cinnamon
- Vegetable oil for frying

How to Prepare

- Mix mashed bananas, all-purpose flour, sugar, baking powder, and ground cinnamon in a bowl.
- Heat vegetable oil in a pan for frying.
- Drop spoonfuls of the batter into the hot oil and fry until golden brown on both sides.
- Remove from the oil and drain on paper towels.
- Enjoy with tea or coffee as dessert or as breakfast!

Storage and Leftovers

Room Temperature: *Store in an airtight container at room temperature for up to 2 days.*

WESTERN AFRICA RECIPES

A brief history of plant-based food in Western Africa

West Africa unfolds its culinary tale through a wealth of traditional plant-based delights, featuring staples like yam, cassava, millet, fonio, plantains, and leafy greens. Starchy wonders like fufu and eba take the spotlight, accompanied by vibrant vegetable-centric soups and stews. Embodied in akara and moi moi, legumes showcase the region's culinary ingenuity, while the tropical climate nurtures an array of fruits, from succulent mangoes to juicy pineapples.

The global impact of West African cuisine echoes in ingredients like okra, black-eyed peas, and yams, journeying across the Atlantic during the Transatlantic Slave Trade and embedding themselves in diaspora cuisines. Today, West Africa seamlessly blends tradition with modernity, embracing plant-based choices fuelled by health consciousness and a renewed fascination with ancestral diets. The result is a mosaic of diverse, delectable, and nutritious plant-based dishes, a vibrant celebration of cultural heritage and agricultural abundance.

Scan for Top-Tier West African Tunes

STREET FOOD

SIDES

SNACKS

Senegalese Accara

These tasty black-eyed pea fritters, crafted with a blend of spices and herbs, are an addictively delicious street food.

Prep Time: 30 minutes
Cook Time: 20 minutes
Total Time: 50 minutes
Difficulty: Intermediate

Ingredients (serves 4)

- 170 g black-eyed peas, soaked and peeled
- 1 onion, chopped
- 2 garlic cloves, minced
- 1 tsp cayenne pepper
- 1 tsp ground black pepper
- 1 tsp baking powder
- Salt to taste
- Vegetable oil for frying

How to Prepare

- Blend peeled black-eyed peas, chopped onions, minced garlic, cayenne pepper, black pepper, baking powder, and salt in a blender. Add a little water if needed to form a thick batter.
- Heat vegetable oil in a deep pan.
- Drop spoonfuls of the batter into the hot oil and fry until golden brown on both sides.

Storage and Leftovers

Room Temperature: *Accara is best enjoyed fresh. If you have leftovers, store them at room temperature for up to 1 day.*

Jollof Rice Balls

A modern twist on the classic of one of the most famous West African dishes of all time: Jollof Rice. This delightful recipe is a great way to refresh leftover J rice and turn it into bite-sized wonders. It's great for dinner parties!

Prep Time: 20 minutes
Cook Time: 30 minutes
Total Time: 50 minutes
Difficulty: Intermediate

Ingredients (serves 4-6)

- Cooked Jollof rice (cooled)
- 75 g flour
- 75 g breadcrumbs
- 75 ml water (add accordingly if needed)
- Vegetable oil (for frying)

How to Prepare

- Take small portions of prepared jollof rice (check out our recipe just after this one) and shape them into balls.
- Combine flour and water to make a wet batter. Add more water if too thick.
- Roll the rice ball in the batter, then in breadcrumbs.
- Heat vegetable oil in a pan and fry the rice balls until golden brown.
- Serve with spicy tomato sauce and enjoy!

Storage and Leftovers

Refrigeration: *Store any leftover Jollof rice balls in an airtight container in the refrigerator for 2–3 days.*

HEARTY MAIN DISHES

Jollof Rice

This timeless West African classic is a delightful fusion of aromatic tomatoey rice that pairs perfectly with fried plantain, grilled veggies, or any meat alternative of your choice! There are many delicious versions across West Africa; this is ours.

Prep Time: 20 minutes
Cook Time: 40 minutes
Total Time: 1 hour
Difficulty: Intermediate

Ingredients (serves 8-10)

- 300 g parboiled rice
- 4 tbsp tomato puree
- 1½ onions, roughly diced
- ½ onion thinly slice
- 4 tomatoes, roughly diced
- 2 bell peppers, roughly diced
- 2 garlic cloves
- 1 scotch bonnet
- 500 ml vegetable stock
- 3–4 thyme sprigs
- 2–3 bay leaves
- 1 rosemary sprig
- 1 thumb of ginger (2–3 cm)
- 2 tsp curry powder
- 1 tbsp smoked paprika
- 1 tbsp chilli powder
- 1½ tbsp all-purpose seasoning
- ½ tbsp white pepper
- Vegetable oil
- Salt and pepper to taste

How to Prepare

- Blend tomato, garlic, ginger, peppers, and scotch bonnet until pureed and set aside.
- Heat the oil, add the thinly sliced onion, and sauté for 1 minute using a large pot, then add the tomato puree and stir.
- Stir all dried seasonings (curry, chilli, all-purpose, white pepper, and paprika) on medium heat for 5–7 minutes.
- Add in the blended mix and stir to combine.
- Place the bay leaves and cover for 30 minutes. The key is to thoroughly cook the stew to give the rice the best flavour.
- Add your parboiled rice to the stew and mix thoroughly covering all of the rice.
- Pour enough stock to almost cover the rice and stir. (You can add more stock later if needed.) Taste if additional salt is needed here.
- Place thyme and rosemary upon the rice and cover with aluminium foil, then the pot lid.
- Stir every 10–15 minutes until the rice is cooked and water is absorbed.
- Use a fork and fluff the rice.
- Serve with raw onion rings for presentation and enjoy with sides of your choice!

Storage and Leftovers

Refrigeration: *Store any leftover Jollof rice in an airtight container in the refrigerator for 2–3 days. Or check out our Jollof Rice Balls.*

Ghanaian Red Red

Discover Ghana's rich and savoury flavours with Red Red, a naturally plant-based, hearty, satisfying bean stew. This traditional Ghanaian dish combines tender black-eyed peas with a tantalising tomato-based sauce, creating a culinary masterpiece that's both comforting and flavourful.

Prep Time: 20 minutes
Cook Time: 45 minutes
Total Time: 1 hour 5 minutes
Difficulty: Moderate

Ingredients (serves 4-6)

- 400 g dried black-eyed peas, soaked overnight
- 4 tomatoes, chopped
- 1 red bell pepper, chopped
- 2 onions, chopped
- 1 scotch bonnet
- 1 thumb-size of fresh ginger
- 2 garlic cloves
- 2 tbsp red palm oil (for authentic flavour)
- 1 tbsp tomato paste
- 1 tsp salt (adjust to taste)
- 1 veg stock cube (alternatively: 2 tsp ground dawadawa or all-purpose seasoning)
- 500 ml vegetable broth

How to Prepare

- Cook the soaked black-eyed peas in salted water in a large pot until tender. Drain and set aside.
- Blend tomatoes, red bell pepper, 1 onion, scotch bonnet, and ginger.
- Heat vegetable oil over medium heat in a separate large pot. Add 1 sliced onion and sauté until translucent.
- Add tomato paste and veg stock cube or alternative spice mentioned above. Stir for 2–3 minutes until fragrant.
- Add the blended paste to the pot, stirring well. Allow the mixture to simmer until the oil begins to separate from the sauce.
- Pour in the vegetable broth, cooked black-eyed peas, salt. Stir to combine, then reduce the heat to low. Simmer for 20–25 minutes until the flavours meld together.
- Garnish with gari (optional), serve with fried plantains and enjoy!

Storage and Leftovers

Refrigerator: *Store any leftover Red Red in an airtight container in the refrigerator for up to 3–4 days.*
Freezer: *Red Red can be frozen in airtight containers for up to 2 months.*

Ivorian Attiéké

Experience the traditional Ivorian Attiéké with a delightful twist featuring mushrooms as an optional, realistic meat replacement! Combined with a fresh salad and fried plantains (locally called Alloco), this recipe creates a harmonious fusion of textures and unique flavours!

Prep Time: 20 minutes
Cook Time: 1 hour
Total Time: 1 hour 20 minutes
Difficulty: Moderate

Ingredients (serves 4)

For Attiéké:

- 400 g cassava couscous (Attiéké)
- 240 ml warm water
- 1 tsp salt

For Mushroom Meat (Optional):

- 10 king oyster mushrooms, finely sliced with heads removed (alternative: cooked jackfruits, oyster mushrooms, or banana blossoms)
- 4 rice paper sheets (for the skin)
- 2 tsp garlic powder
- 2 tbsp all-purpose seasoning
- 2 tsp mixed herbs
- 1 tsp paprika
- 2 tsp mushroom marinade (see below)

For Mushroom Meat Marinate:

- 75 g green pepper, chopped
- 75 g red pepper, chopped
- 35 g spring onion, chopped
- 10 g coriander, chopped
- 35 g parsley, chopped
- 10 g ginger, chopped
- 7 garlic cloves, chopped

How to Prepare

Prepare Mushroom Meat Marinade:

- In a food processor, blend green and red peppers, spring onions, coriander, parsley, ginger, garlic cloves, mint leaves, bay leaves, black pepper, salt, mustard, paprika, lemon juice, and oil.

Prepare Mushrooms Meat:

- Slice the mushrooms into very thin slices.
- Boil the mushrooms with garlic powder, all-purpose seasoning, mixed herbs, and 1 tsp of the marinade for about 10 minutes. Drain the mushrooms and pat with a kitchen towel.
- Dip the rice paper in water for a few seconds until pliable.
- Carefully assemble the slices at the centre of the rice paper and layer them up to the desired thickness. Wrap tight.
- Brush with the marinade made previously, and sprinkle some paprika.
- Roast for 15–20 minutes at 190°C.

Prepare Alloco:

- Fry plantains in vegetable oil until golden brown on both sides.
- Remove and place on a paper towel to absorb excess oil.

Prepare Tomato Sauce:

- Blend tomatoes, onions, and garlic in a food processor to create a sauce.
- Heat oil over low heat and add the sauce in a pot.
- Add tomato paste and season with all-purpose seasoning and black pepper.
- Let simmer for 5–10 minutes.

- 3 mint leaves, chopped
- 2 bay leaves
- 1 tsp of black pepper
- 1 tsp of salt
- 1 tbsp mustard
- 1 tsp paprika
- ½ lemon juice
- 2 tbsp groundnut oil

For Fresh Salad:

- 2 tomatoes, diced (without seeds)
- 1 cucumber, diced (without seeds)
- 2 white onions, diced
- 3 tbsp groundnut oil
- 1 tbsp apple vinegar (or white vinegar)
- 1 tsp salt
- 1 tsp black pepper
- 1 tsp mustard (optional)
- 1 fresh green chili, diced (optional)

For Tomato Sauce:

- 1 large tomato, chopped into wedges
- 1 large white onion, chopped into wedges
- 5 garlic cloves
- 1 tsp tomato paste
- 2 tsp groundnut oil
- 1 tsp all-purpose seasoning
- 1 tsp black pepper

For Alloco (Fried Plantains):

- 4 ripe plantains, peeled and sliced into preferred shape
- Vegetable oil for frying
- Salt to taste

Prepare Attiéké:

- Pour Attiéké into a container and sprinkle with cold water. Stir with a fork.
- Place the wet Attiéké on a couscous steamer. Put it on top of the pot containing boiling water. Cover and steam for 8–10 minutes.
- Fluff Attiéké with a fork to separate the grains.

Prepare Fresh Salad:

- Mix diced tomatoes, onions, and cucumbers in a bowl.
- Add olive oil, apple vinegar, salt, and black pepper. If using mustard and green chilli, add them here. Stir well and set aside.

Storage and Leftovers

Refrigeration: *Store Attiéké and sautéed oyster mushrooms separately in airtight containers in the refrigerator for up to 3–4 days.*

Nigerian Okra Soup with Fufu

This traditional dish marries the deliciously slimy texture of okra with the comforting texture of fufu. This culinary delight offers a taste of Nigeria's vibrant and diverse gastronomy, making every handful a journey of savoury satisfaction.

Prep Time: 20 minutes
Cook Time: 30 minutes
Total Time: 50 minutes
Difficulty: Intermediate

Ingredients (serves 4-6)

For Okra Soup:

- 500 g okra, chopped
- 1 onion, finely chopped
- 2 tomatoes, diced
- 2 bell peppers, diced
- 150 g spinach, chopped
- 1 scotch bonnet
- 450 ml stock, either 3 meat-free beef stock cubes or vegetable
- 2 tbsp palm oil
- Salt and pepper to taste
- Optional meat alternative additions: tempeh chunks or canned jackfruit chunks (be aware fresh takes longer to cook)
- Optional seasoning: Iru (fermented locust beans), Uziza powder, nori powder (for crayfish alternative) – use 1–2 tsp for each, mindful these each has a strong flavour

For Fufu:

- 300 g fufu flour or another preferred swallow
- 1 L of water

How to Prepare

Prepare Okra Soup:

- Blend tomatoes, peppers, and scotch bonnet until pureed, then set aside.
- Use an additional pot, if using tempeh or jackfruit chunks, with some stock to cover and cook until tender and absorb all the flavours.
- Melt the palm oil and sauté chopped onions in a pot until soft.
- Add in the blended tomato mix and cook for 5–7 minutes. Our suggested optional seasoning can be added here.
- Add the chopped okra, spinach, stock, and cover. Simmer until the okra is cooked. This will be soft with a pleasantly slimy texture (approx. 15–20 minutes). If you wish for the consistency to be less slimy, do not cover the pot completely (but we wouldn't recommend it).
- Add the cooked tempeh or jackfruit here and mix in (optional).
- Serve hot with fufu or rice of your choice!

Prepare Fufu:

- Using a large pot, bring 1 L of water to a boil. Whilst on the heat, add the fufu flour and mix well using a wooden spoon to avoid lumps.
- The fufu is ready when it is smooth and thickens into a dough. Add more water or fufu flour if required. Shape into a ball to serve.

Storage and Leftovers

Refrigeration: *Store any leftover okra soup and fufu separately in airtight containers in the refrigerator for up to 2–3 days.*

West African Maafe

This vegan adaptation of the traditional West African dish, Maafe, paired with rice (or fonio), combines hearty vegetables, peanut butter, and aromatic spices for a flavourful and satisfying plant-based meal. We love our Maafe this way, but if you would like to add a meat alternative, we recommend adding some jackfruit or tempeh chunks.

Prep Time: 20 minutes
Cook Time: 40 minutes
Total Time: 1 hour
Difficulty: Moderate

Ingredients (serves 4)

For vegetables:

- 1 large sweet potato, cut in chunks
- 2 carrots, cut in chunks
- Optional meat alternative: oyster mushrooms or canned jackfruit chunks (be aware fresh takes longer to cook)

For stew:

- 2 tbsp peanut oil
- 1 large onion, chopped
- 3 tbsp tomato paste
- 1/2 can of tomato
- 500 ml vegetable broth
- 4 tbsp peanut butter, melted
- 1 tbsp dawadawa for umami flavour
- 1 tbsp all-purpose seasoning
- 1 tsp paprika (optional)
- 1 tsp chilli powder (optional)

For nokoss: (green marinade)

- A handful of parsley
- A handful of spring onions
- ½ green bell pepper
- 1 red onion, chopped
- 1 scotch bonnet
- 4 garlic cloves, chopped
- 3 bay leaves &1 tsp salt
- 1 tbsp black pepper

How to Prepare

Prepare Nokoss:

- In a mortar or a food processor, grind parsley, spring onion, bell pepper, onion, scotch bonnet, garlic cloves, bay leaves, salt, and black pepper.

Prepare Stew:

- Sauté the onion in a pot with oil until translucent.
- Add tomato paste, dawadawa, all-purpose seasoning, paprika, and chilli powder. Stir well and let cook for 3–5 minutes, stirring occasionally.
- Add nokoss, canned tomatoes, and vegetable broth. Mix well. Add salt and pepper if needed.
- Add sweet potato, carrots, and optional meat alternative. Let cook until tender.
- Add melted peanut butter and stir well. Let it cook for about 20–30 minutes, stirring occasionally, until the oil rises to the surface.
- Serve maafe over a bed of cooked rice or fonio and enjoy!

Storage and Leftovers

Refrigeration: *Refrigerate any leftover Maafe in an airtight container for up to 3–4 days. Rice can be stored separately and reheated as needed. Reheat the Maafe on the stovetop or in the microwave.*

Nigerian Egusi Soup and Pounded Yam

This vegan adaptation of the traditional Nigerian dish, egusi soup, paired with pounded yam, brings together the rich flavours of egusi seeds, vegetables, and aromatic spices for a delicious and satisfying plant-based meal. We love our egusi soup this way, but if you would like to add an additional meat alternative, we recommend adding some tempeh or jackfruit chunks!

Prep Time: 20 minutes
Cook Time: 40 minutes
Total Time: 1 hour
Difficulty: Moderate

Ingredients (serves 4)

For the Egusi Soup:

- 200 g egusi (melon seeds), ground
- 2 tbsp red palm oil
- 1 onion, finely chopped
- 3 garlic cloves, minced
- 1 scotch bonnet pepper, finely chopped
- 300 g spinach or bitter leaves (thoroughly washed to remove bitterness), chopped
- 300 g oyster mushrooms (alternative: tempeh chunks, canned jackfruit chunks, chestnut mushrooms), roughly chopped for meaty texture
- 3 meat-free beef stock cubes or vegetable
- 750 ml broth (see below)
- 1½ tsp of smoked paprika
- 1 tsp of garlic powder
- 1½ tsp of all-purpose seasoning

How to Prepare

Prepare the Broth:

- Combine chopped mushrooms, paprika, garlic powder, and all-purpose seasoning in a large pot, then add enough water to cover. Boil for 10–15 minutes, then set mushrooms aside. Add in stock cubes and remove from heat.

Prepare the Egusi Soup:

- Melt down the palm oil over a medium heat. Once melted, add onions and sauté until translucent.
- Then add garlic cloves and chopped scotch bonnet pepper. Add our optional seasoning here if using, and allow to cook.
- Add the mushrooms previously set aside and cook for 5–7 minutes.
- If using tempeh or jackfruit chunks, use an additional pot using broth to cover and cook until tender and has absorbed all the flavours.
- Add the ground egusi, chopped spinach, or bitter leaves, and stir well.
- Pour in the broth and bring the mixture to a gentle boil, then cover and simmer for 5–10 minutes. Add additional broth if too thick for the preferred consistency. Add the cooked tempeh or jackfruit here and mix in (optional).
- Season the soup with salt and pepper. Adjusting the seasoning to taste.

- Salt and pepper to taste
- Optional seasoning: Iru (fermented locust beans), Uziza powder, nori powder (dried mushrooms and nori ground together for a crayfish alternative) – use 1–2 tsp for each, mindful these each has a strong flavour

For the Pounded Yam:

- 480 g pounded yam flour or another preferred swallow
- 1 L of water

For the Pounded Yam:

- Using a large pot, bring 1 L of water to a boil. Whilst on the heat, add the yam flour and mix well using a wooden spoon to avoid lumps.
- The yam is ready when it is smooth and thickens into a dough. Add more water or yam flour if required. Shape into a ball to serve.
- Serve the pounded yam alongside the egusi soup.

Storage and Leftovers

Refrigeration: *Refrigerate any leftover egusi soup in an airtight container for up to 3–4 days. Pounded yam is best enjoyed fresh but can be stored in the refrigerator for up to 2 days. Reheat the soup on the stovetop or in the microwave.*

Senegalese Thiéboudienne

Welcome to the heart of Senegal! This iconic national treasure embodies Senegal's rich cultural heritage. Traditionally made with fish, we recommend to simply embrace the harmonious blend of flavours from the vegs!

Prep Time: 30 minutes
Cook Time: 1 hour
Total Time: 1 hour 30 minutes
Difficulty: Intermediate

Ingredients (serves 4)

For rice:

- 500 g broken rice, washed

For vegetables:

- ½ head of white cabbage
- 1 aubergine, chopped in half
- 1 carrots, whole
- 1 sweet potato, chopped in large chunks
- Lime slices, for serving

For Nokoss (Senegalese green seasoning for marinades):

- 3 tbsp fresh parsley, chopped
- 1 tbsp spring onion, chopped
- 1 green bell pepper, chopped
- 1 onion, chopped
- 1 scotch bonnet, chopped
- 5 garlic cloves, chopped
- 3 bay leaves
- 2 tbsp ground nori sheets (for fish flavour)
- 1 veg stock cube
- 1 tbsp dawadawa or all-purpose seasoning for umiami flavour
- 1 tsp black pepper
- 1 tsp salt

How to Prepare

Prepare Nokoss:

- In a mortar or a food processor, grind parsley, spring onion, bell pepper, onion, scotch bonnet, garlic cloves, bay leaves, nori sheets, veg stock cube, dawadawa, black pepper, and salt.

Prepare Stew:

- Sauté the onion until it starts to brown in a large pot with oil.
- Add tomato paste, veg stock cube, ground nori sheets, dawadawa or all-purpose seasoning, salt, and pepper. Stir well and let cook for 5 minutes, stirring occasionally.
- Add nokoss, blended tomatoes, and vegetable broth. Mix well and let cook for about 30 minutes on medium heat until the oil rises to the top, stirring occasionally. Add salt and pepper if needed.
- Set aside some of the stew to sprinkle on plate later.
- Add some water, cabbage, aubergine, carrots, and sweet potatoes. Let cook until tender.
- Take out the vegetables and set aside.

For Stew:

- 20 cl vegetable oil
- 2 onions, chopped
- 4 tbsp tomato paste
- 5 tomatoes, blended
- 500 ml vegetable broth
- 1 veg stock cube
- 1 tbsp dawadawa or all-purpose seasoning for umiami flavour
- 1 tbsp ground nori sheets (to replace guedj and yet for fish flavour)
- 1 tsp salt to taste
- 1 tsp black pepper to taste

Prepare Rice:

- Using a couscous steamer, steam the rice for about 15 minutes to pre-cook it.
- Add the pre-cooked rice into the stew.
- Once the stew is absorbed, reduce to low heat and cover the pot with a lid on top. Let cook for about 15 minutes.
- Stir the rice and let cook for another 5–10 minutes.
- Place the rice on a large serving tray, cover it with vegetables and lime, pour some stew previously set aside and enjoy!

Storage and Leftovers

Refrigeration: *Store any leftover Thiéboudienne in an airtight container in the refrigerator for up to 2–3 days.*

DELICIOUS DESSERTS

Senegalese Caakiri

Indulge in the delightful experience of Senegalese Caakiri, a luscious dessert harmonising millet couscous with yoghurt. This sweet treat encapsulates the rich textures and sweet traditions that embody Senegalese culinary excellence.

Prep Time: 20 minutes
Cook Time: 30 minutes
Total Time: 50 minutes
Difficulty: Intermediate

Ingredients (serves 4)

Millet:

- 200 g Millet couscous
- 1 tbsp plant-based butter

Porridge:

- 500 g plain plant-based yogurt
- 400 ml plant-based milk
- 70 g sugar (to taste)
- 1 tsp vanilla extract (to taste)
- 1 tsp ground nutmeg
- 1 tsp ground cinnamon
- Coconut flakes (optional for garnish)

How to Prepare

Prepare Millet:

- In a large bowl, add millet couscous.
- Add enough boiling water to cover the couscous. Cover the bowl and leave it for about 5 minutes until fluffy. (Alternatively, you can cook it in microwave for 3–5 minutes.)
- Add plant-based butter and mix well.

Prepare Porridge:

- In a pot, combine plant-based milk, plant-based yogurt, sugar, vanilla extract, nutmeg, and cinnamon. Stir continuously until it thickens like a porridge consistency.
- Pour the Caakiri into serving bowls and garnish with coconut flakes if desired.

Storage and Leftovers

Refrigeration: *Store any leftover Caakiri in an airtight container in the refrigerator for up to 2–3 days.*

Ghanaian Peanut Brittle

This traditional treat showcases the perfect balance of roasted peanuts and caramelised sugar. Every bite of this irresistible snack offers a tasty experience of opulent flavours and delightful textures.

Prep Time: 15 minutes
Cook Time: 15 minutes
Total Time: 30 minutes
Difficulty: Easy

Ingredients (serves 6)

- 165 g peanuts, roasted and roughly chopped
- 200 g sugar
- 125 ml water
- 2 tbsp plant-based butter
- ½ tsp vanilla extract
- ¼ tsp baking soda

How to Prepare

- Line a baking sheet with parchment paper and set aside.
- In a saucepan, combine sugar and water. Cook over medium heat until the sugar dissolves.
- Stir in roasted peanuts and continue cooking, stirring frequently, until the mixture reaches a golden brown.
- Remove the saucepan from heat and quickly stir in vegan butter, vanilla extract, and baking soda.
- Pour the mixture onto the prepared baking sheet and spread it out evenly. Let it cool and harden.
- Once completely cooled, break the peanut brittle into bite-sized pieces.

Storage and Leftovers

Room Temperature: *Store peanut brittle in an airtight container at room temperature for up to 1–2 weeks.*

NORTHERN AFRICA RECIPES

A brief history of plant-based food in North Africa

Embark on a culinary journey through North Africa, where the roots of plant-based eating run deep, tracing back thousands of years. In ancient civilisations like the Egyptians or Kemets, grains, vegetables, and fruits took centre stage, with bread as a dietary cornerstone. The indigenous Amazigh people thrived on staples like couscous and argan oil, embodying a rich plant-based tradition. Islamic dietary practices, particularly during Ramadan, further emphasise plant-based choices. The region's historic trade routes facilitated the exchange of spices, creating a diverse culinary tapestry.

North Africa's plant-based culinary legacy is a story of resilience and adaptation to its unique geography. From ancient civilisations to contemporary sustainability movements, the region's cuisine remains deeply rooted in its bountiful plant-based ingredients, showcasing a flavourful fusion of tradition and modernity.

Scan for Impeccable North African Vibes

STREET FOOD SIDES SNACKS

Algerian Mahjouba

This stuffed flatbread is a savoury delicacy often found sold on the streets of Algeria. Thin layers of golden, flaky flatbread are filled with a delightful mixture of traditional spices to create crispy, rich, and flavourful bites.

Prep Time: 10 minutes and 30 minutes of resting time
Cooking Time: 45 minutes
Total Time: 1 hour 25 minutes
Difficulty Level: Easy

Ingredients (serves 6)

For the Dough:

- 250 g fine semolina
- 1 tsp salt
- 1 tbsp oil (plus more for greasing)
- Water (as needed to make the dough)

How to Prepare

Prepare the Dough:

- Combine the semolina flour and salt in a bowl and mix them together.
- Slowly add water to make a soft dough. Knead the dough for 6–8 minutes until it is elastic. Make sure the dough is not too wet or not too dry.
- Add 1 tbsp of oil and continue to knead. Let the dough rest for at least 30 minutes.
- The longer the dough rests, the more flexible it is to use later!

Prepare the Filling:

- Heat 1 tbsp of oil in a pan. Add the finely chopped onions when the oil is hot and sauté until translucent.
- Add the cumin and paprika and let them simmer with the onions until fragrant (3–5 minutes). Do not let the spices burn.
- Add the grated carrot and sauté for a couple of minutes.
- Add the green chillies, chopped tomatoes, and tomato paste and let everything come to a boil.
- Add the salt and pepper. If the canned tomatoes already have salt, just add enough to taste.
- Simmer and let the mixture thicken. It will take 15–20 minutes to get the right consistency.
- Let the filling cool down before starting to assemble the Mahjouba.

For the Filling:

- 1 onion finely chopped
- 5 chopped tomatoes (or 1 tin)
- 2 tbsp of tomato paste
- 1 finely grated carrot
- 2 or 3 green chillies, finely chopped
- 1 tsp cumin
- 1 tsp paprika
- 1 tbsp oil
- Salt and pepper to taste

Prepares the Mahjouba:

- Divide the dough into 6 equal balls. Coat each piece with oil and place it on a greased surface.
- Spread the ball with the heel of your hand to form a very thin circle. Try not to tear the dough as you do this.
- Stretch the edges and make the dough as thin as possible. It must be well kneaded and rested so it does not tear much. Also make sure the surface is well greased, as well as your hands to avoid tearing.
- Spread about 2 heaped tbsp of the filling in the centre and fold the 2 opposite ends to meet at the centre.
- Now, fold the other 2 ends to the centre and form an envelope.
- Heat a flat griddle or pan and spray it with some oil.
- Place the shaped Mahjouba on the hot pan and cook it on both sides until golden brown.
- Repeat the same with the rest of the dough.
- Let it cool slightly, and then serve.

Storage and Leftovers

Refrigeration: *If stored properly, mahjouba will keep well in the fridge for 2–3 days. Allow it to cool before you cover it and put it in the fridge.*

Freezing: *It is not ideal to freeze mahjouba as it is best eaten fresh.*

Reheating: *When ready to enjoy your leftovers, reheat the mahjouba in a pan on medium heat with some oil until heated.*

Kabylie-Style Spicy Potatoes

Elevate the humble potato into a spicy sensation. These tender spuds are infused with the vibrant essence of Kabyle, an Amazigh region in Algeria, turning each bite into a flavourful adventure and a celebration of indigenous North African culture.

Prep Time: 15 minutes
Cooking Time: 1 hour
Total Time: 1 hour 15 minutes
Difficulty Level: Easy

Ingredients (serves 6-8)

- 1 kg white potatoes, cut into cubes
- 2 tomatoes, cut into cubes
- 1–2 green or red peppers, cut into cubes
- 2–3 garlic cloves, minced
- 2 onions, chopped
- 1 chilli
- 1 handful of olives
- 1 handful fresh parsley
- 1 handful fresh coriander
- 1 tsp ras el hanout spice (see Herbs and Spices section for exact mix)
- Salt and black pepper, to taste
- Hot paprika, to taste

How to Prepare

- Clean and cut all your vegetables.
- Fry the potatoes in oil, air-fry, or bake until crispy.
- Sauté the onions in some olive oil in a pan.
- Add garlic, chilli, peppers, and tomatoes, and sauté for a few minutes.
- Add the rest of the spices and potatoes, and sauté for a few minutes.
- Add the olives and fresh herbs and mix in well before serving.

Storage and Leftovers

Refrigeration: *If stored properly, batata harra will keep well in the fridge for 3–4 days. Allow to cool before you transfer it to a container with a tight lid.*

Freezing: *You can also freeze batata harra in a freezer-safe container or an airtight freezer bag, removing as much air as possible to prevent freezer burn. It can be frozen for up to 12 months.*

Reheating: *When ready to enjoy your leftovers, reheat them in a pan over low to medium heat until the batata harra is heated. You may need to add a little oil to refresh the potatoes. If reheating from frozen, allow the potatoes to thaw before applying a little oil and reheat in the oven until the potatoes are heated.*

Moroccan Zaalouk

This aubergine salad invites you to savour the essence of Morocco in every bite. Experience the medley of smoky roasted aubergine, ripe tomatoes, and aromatic spices that pair gorgeously with any bread of your choice.

Prep Time: 20 minutes
Cooking Time: 25 minutes
Total Time: 45 minutes
Difficulty Level: Easy

Ingredients (serves up to 6)

- Cooked Jollof rice (cooled)
- 75 g breadcrumbs
- Vegetable oil (for frying)

How to Prepare

- Place the aubergine cubes in a colander and toss with a good pinch of salt. Set aside a few minutes while you prepare the rest of the ingredients. When ready to cook, wipe the aubergine dry, removing excess salt.
- In a large non-stick pan with a lid, heat about 2 tbsp extra virgin olive oil, and add the aubergine, diced tomatoes, and minced garlic.
- Season with salt, cumin, paprika, and chilli flakes. Toss around for about 5 minutes, then add a handful of chopped coriander and parsley with about 5 tbsp of water.
- Bring the mixture to a boil, then turn the heat down. Cover the pan with the lid and allow the eggplant and tomatoes to simmer until very tender for about 20 minutes. Ensure to occasionally check and stir so nothing sticks to the pan, adding more water if needed.
- Stir in the lemon juice once the aubergine and tomatoes are very tender. Use a potato masher or the back of a fork to gently mash to your desired consistency (some people like it very smooth, others prefer it chunky).
- Remove from heat. Transfer the zaalouk to a serving bowl. You can serve it warm or allow it to cool to room temperature. You can also refrigerate it to serve later.
- Top the zaalouk with a good drizzle of extra virgin olive oil, fresh coriander, and a dash of chilli flakes when ready to serve. Serve with pita bread or your favourite bread of choice.

Storage and Leftovers

Refrigeration: *If stored properly, zaalouk will keep well in the fridge for 4–5 days. Allow the salad to cool before you transfer it to a glass container with a tight lid. Adding a drizzle of olive oil to cover the top will help seal it.*

Freezing: *You can also freeze zaalouk for longer storage. Place it in a freezer-safe container or an airtight freezer bag, removing as much air as possible to prevent freezer burn. It can be frozen for up to 2–3 months.*

Reheating: *It is not necessary to reheat this salad as some enjoy it cold; however, simply add the zaalouk to a pan until heated through, if desired, hot. If reheating from frozen, thaw overnight and reheat in a pan to freshen it up and reduce any excess liquid.*

Tunisian Shakshouka

Indulge in the warmth of Shakshuka, a well-known delight that makes breakfast the best part of your day. Immerse yourself in a rich tomato and bell pepper stew, gently cradling perfectly cooked tofu eggs that will make your taste buds dance with joy.

Prep time: 20 minutes
Cooking time: 30 minutes
Total time: 50 minutes
Difficulty level: Easy

Ingredients (serves up to 4)

For the Shakshuka Sauce:

- 2 tbsp extra virgin olive oil
- 1 onion, diced
- 2 bell peppers, diced
- 4 garlic cloves, minced
- 1 can chopped tomatoes
- 2 tsp cumin
- 2 tsp ground smoked paprika
- 1 tsp cayenne pepper (adjust to your spice preference)
- Salt and black pepper to taste
- 1 tsp sugar (optional, to balance acidity)
- 1 handful of coriander or parsley, chopped (for garnish)

For the Tofu 'Eggs':

- 300 g silken tofu
- 1 tsp ground turmeric
- 2 tsp black salt (Kala Namak for egg flavour)
- 1 tsp white pepper
- 1 tsp nutritional yeast
- 1 tbsp lemon juice

How to Prepare

- Start by preparing the tofu 'eggs'. Blend tofu, black salt, nutritional yeast, white pepper, and lemon juice until you have a paste. The mixture should not be liquid.
- Heat the olive oil over medium heat in a large skillet or frying pan. Add the diced onion and bell peppers. Sauté for about 5–7 minutes, or until they become soft and slightly caramelised.
- Add the minced garlic and sauté for another 1–2 minutes until fragrant, being careful not to burn it.
- Stir in the ground cumin, paprika, cayenne pepper, salt, and black pepper. Cook for 2 minutes to toast the spices and enhance their flavours.
- Pour in the crushed tomatoes and stir well to combine. If the mixture is too thick, add a water splash to achieve your desired consistency. Add sugar if the tomatoes are too acidic for your taste.
- Allow the tomato mixture to simmer over low heat for 10–15 minutes or until the sauce thickens and the flavours meld together.
- Create small wells in the sauce with a spoon and carefully place the tofu 'egg' mixture into the wells. Cook for 5–7 minutes until the tofu is heated through. Do not mix after this step.
- Sprinkle fresh coriander or parsley over the top for garnish.
- Serve your Shakshuka hot, straight from the skillet. You can enjoy it with crusty bread, pita, or even rice.

Storage and Leftovers

Refrigeration: *Allow any leftover shakshuka to cool to room temperature. Transfer it to an airtight container and refrigerate. It should stay fresh in the refrigerator for 3–4 days.*

Freezing: *You can also freeze shakshuka for longer storage. Place it in a freezer-safe container or an airtight freezer bag, removing as much air as possible to prevent freezer burn. It can be frozen for up to 2–3 months.*

Reheating: *When you're ready to enjoy your leftovers, reheat them on the stovetop over low to medium heat until the shakshuka is heated. You may need to add a little water or vegetable broth to adjust the consistency if it has thickened during storage.*

HEARTY MAIN DISHES

Algerian Couscous with Vegetables

Delight in the light, fluffy couscous grains, meticulously paired with an array of vibrant vegetables, offering a taste of North African tradition that's both comforting and delicious.

Prep Time: 30 minutes
Cooking Time: 45 minutes
Total Time: 1 hour and 15 minutes
Difficulty Level: Intermediate

Ingredients (serves up to 4)

For the Semolina:

- 250 g medium-grain semolina
- Olive oil
- Salt
- Plant-based butter

For the Couscous Sauce:

- 1 tbsp olive oil
- 2 onions, chopped
- 3 carrots, cut into large chunks
- 4 tomatoes, cut into large chunks
- 2 courgettes, cut into large chunks
- Any other seasonal vegetable, such as potato or suede
- 1 can of chickpeas
- 3 tbsp of tomato paste
- 1 tbsp of harissa (depending on spice preference)
- 500 ml of water
- 1 bay leaf
- 2 tsp paprika
- 1 tsp cinnamon
- 1 tsp nutmeg
- 1 tsp turmeric

How to Prepare

- This recipe traditionally uses a couscoussier (a deep saucepan with a steamer that fits on top); however, a deep saucepan and separate steamer will also work.
- Heat the oil on medium heat and add the onion, salt, and bay leaf in the bottom part of a couscoussier (or a large saucepan). Sauté until the onion has browned slightly (around 5–6 minutes).
- Add the remaining vegetables, tomato paste, passata, and spices and mix well for about 2 minutes.
- Add the water, lower the heat and add the top steamer with the lid to let it heat up. Give the sauce a quick stir every 10 minutes.
- Place the semolina in a colander and run under warm water while the vegetables are cooking. Then, transfer the semolina to a bowl and mix in salt and olive oil.
- Put the semolina in the top of the couscoussier (the top steamer part) and place the lid on, letting it steam for about 10 minutes.
- Return the semolina to the same bowl and add the butter. Now rub the semolina between your palms to separate the grains and cover each one in butter. Then return to the couscoussier and steam for another 10 minutes.
- Repeat the last 2 steps until your desired couscous texture (3–4 times should do it).
- Place the semolina on a large platter and top it off with the sauce while serving. Add some harissa and a drizzle of olive oil if you like spice. This meal is traditionally enjoyed between groups of people eating from the same platter.

- 2 tsp ras el hanout (see Herbs and Spices section for exact mix)
- Salt and pepper to taste

Storage and Leftovers

Refrigeration: *If stored properly, batata harra will keep well in the fridge for 3–4 days. Allow to cool before you transfer it to a container with a tight lid.*

Freezing: *You can also freeze batata harra in a freezer-safe container or an airtight freezer bag, removing as much air as possible to prevent freezer burn. It can be frozen for up to 12 months.*

Reheating: *When ready to enjoy your leftovers, reheat them in a pan over low to medium heat until the batata harra is heated. You may need to add a little oil to refresh the potatoes. If reheating from frozen, allow the potatoes to thaw.*

Moroccan Tajine

Savour tender, slow-cooked vegetables, bathed in a fragrant blend of spices, creating a delectable masterpiece that embodies Moroccan cuisine's rich and aromatic essence.

Prep Time: 20 minutes
Cook Time: 40 minutes
Total Time: 1 hour
Difficulty: Easy

Ingredients (serves 4)

- 330 g chickpeas, cooked
- 1 large aubergine, diced
- 2 carrots, sliced
- 1 onion, chopped
- 5 garlic cloves, minced
- 1 cup cherry tomatoes, halved
- 100 g apricots or prunes, chopped
- 50 g raisins (optional)
- 1 tbsp tomato paste
- 2 tsp ground cumin
- 2 tsp ground coriander
- 1 tsp ground cinnamon
- 1 tsp smoked paprika
- Salt and pepper to taste
- 3 tbsp olive oil
- 1 handful fresh coriander for garnish
- Juice of ½ a lemon

How to Prepare

- In a tajine or large pot, sauté onions and garlic in olive oil until softened.
- Add the aubergine, carrots, chickpeas, cherry tomatoes, apricots or prunes, and raisins. Stir well.
- Mix in tomato paste, cumin, coriander, cinnamon, smoked paprika, salt, and pepper.
- Pour enough water to cover the ingredients, cover the tajine, and simmer until vegetables are tender (about 30–40 minutes).
- Garnish with fresh coriander and lemon juice before serving with bread of your choice.

Storage and Leftovers

Refrigeration: *After relishing the delightful Moroccan Tajine, let it cool to room temperature before storing. Put the sauce in an air-tight container. This plant-based Tajine can retain its flavours in the fridge for up to 3–4 days.*

Freezing: *Allow the entire dish to cool to room temperature. Portion the sauce out and place it in an airtight container. Frozen, it can be stored for up to 2–3 months.*

Reheating: *When it's time to enjoy your leftovers from the fridge or freezer, here's how to reheat them to perfection. If reheating from the fridge, warm the Tajine in a saucepan or microwave, adding olive oil until it's piping hot. For frozen portions, allow them to thaw in the fridge overnight, and then reheat as you would from the fridge, adding olive oil or water if needed. This ensures that your Tajine is as delicious as the day it was made.*

Libyan Bazeen

This hearty blend of wheat and barley flours, expertly kneaded into a dense, flavourful dough and served alongside a savoury stew resonates with the warmth and authenticity of Libyan culture. We love Bazeen meatless, but we recommend adding tofu chunks or mushrooms into the mix if you want a meat alternative!

Prep Time: 20 minutes
Cook Time: 40 minutes
Total Time: 1 hour
Difficulty: Intermediate

Ingredients (serves 4)

For the Sauce:

- 2 tbsp olive oil
- 1 onion diced
- 2–3 tbsp of tomato paste
- 1 tbsp fenugreek seeds
- 1 tbsp cayenne pepper
- 1 tbsp turmeric
- Salt to taste
- 4 potatoes, halved
- 4 cups of boiling water
- 1 can of chickpeas

For the Dough:

- 350 g barley flour
- 450 ml water

How to Prepare

Prepare the Sauce:

- Heat the olive oil in a large saucepan and sauté the diced onion until tender.
- Add the tomato paste and mix well for 5 minutes. Lower the heat if needed.
- Add the chickpeas, fenugreek seeds, cayenne pepper, turmeric, and salt. Mix well and cook for another 5 minutes.
- Add about 4 cups of boiling water and stir well to ensure everything is well mixed.
- Bring the sauce to a boil and add the potatoes.
- Let simmer until everything is cooked through, then turn off the heat.

Prepare the Dough:

- Mix the barley flour in a large bowl and slowly but surely add the water as you mix by hand.
- There are different methods to make the dough, but mixing everything by hand is the easiest.
- Mix until you have a smooth, sticky, and soft dough. It will firm up once cooked.
- Bring salted water to a boil and break off large chunks of the dough.
- If you poke holes in each chunk of dough, they will cook quicker and more evenly.
- Stir the dough pieces around to ensure they don't stick to the bottom of the pan.
- After about 20 minutes, the dough chunks will float and get a bit puffy. Save some of the dough water and drain the rest.

- Ask someone to hold the pot of dough still and break up the dough using a long wooden spoon or stick. Add some of the previously removed water and keep breaking up the dough chunks.
- Smooth the dough around the edges of the pot until you have a smooth, thick dough paste. This is Bazeen, a firm dough.
- Add the Bazeen to a clean surface and knead until there are no lumps. Then roll into a large, smooth ball.
- Keep rolling until you get a cone shape as you roll the dough into a ball.
- Then place the dough cone in a large serving dish and press it down so it stays in place.
- Dip it in the sauce and create a crevice in the dough cone, so it kind of looks like a volcano.
- Evenly dish the sauce around the Bazeen dough cone in the large serving dish.
- Bazeen is a communal dish eaten with hands. So enjoy with friends and family!

Storage and Leftovers

Refrigeration: *Allow the Bazeen to cool, then transfer to an airtight container. Refrigerate for up to 3–4 days.*

Freezing: *Bazeen is best enjoyed fresh, and it is best not to freeze.*

Reheating: *Reheat the sauce on the stovetop over medium heat, stirring occasionally. Reheat the dough in the microwave for no more than 2 minutes.*

Egyptian Koshari

Experience the heart of Egyptian street food with Koshari – a flavourful fusion of lentils, rice, pasta, and crispy onions, topped with tangy tomato sauce and garlic vinegar. This beloved dish is a culinary symphony that captures the essence of Egyptian tradition.

Prep Time: 20 minutes
Cook Time: 30 minutes
Total Time: 50 minutes
Difficulty: Easy

Ingredients (serves 4)

- 400 g green lentils
- 500 g rice
- 175 g cooked chickpeas
- 100 g pasta (macaroni or penne)
- 1 onion, thinly sliced
- 3 garlic cloves, minced
- 2 tbsp distilled white vinegar
- 1 can crushed tomatoes
- 2 tbsp tomato paste
- 1 tsp ground cumin
- 1 tsp ground coriander
- 1 tsp cayenne pepper
- Salt and pepper to taste
- 3 tbsp olive oil
- Fried onions for garnish

How to Prepare

Prepare the Sauce:

- Heat 1 tbsp olive oil in a saucepan. Add the onion and cook on medium-high until the onion turns translucent. Now add the garlic, coriander, cumin, cayenne pepper, and sauté briefly until fragrant (30–45 seconds more).
- Stir in tomato sauce and a pinch of salt. Bring to a simmer and cook for around 15 minutes, until the sauce thickens.
- Stir in the distilled white vinegar, and turn the heat to low. Cover and keep warm until ready to serve.

Prepare the Koshari:

- Cook the lentils by bringing them and 4 cups of water to a boil in a medium pot or saucepan over high heat. Once boiling, reduce the heat to low and simmer for 15 minutes, until the lentils are just tender. Drain the lentils and season them with a pinch of salt. The lentils should be par-cooked, retaining a slight bite, as they will finish cooking with the rice.
- Drain the soaked rice and combine it with the par-cooked lentils in the saucepan over medium-high heat. Add 1 tbsp of olive oil, salt, pepper, and coriander. Cook for 3 minutes, stirring regularly. Pour boiling water into the saucepan, covering the rice and lentil mixture by about 1½ inches (approximately 3 cups of water). Bring to a boil, allowing the water to reduce slightly. Cover the saucepan and cook for 15–20 minutes until all the liquid is absorbed and the rice and lentils are thoroughly cooked. Keep covered and undisturbed for an additional 5–10 minutes. Then fluff with a fork.

- As the rice and lentils cook, prepare the pasta. Follow the package instructions, boiling the pasta in salted water with a dash of oil until al dente. Drain the pasta, but save the pasta water.
- Using the pasta water, boil the chickpeas for around 5 minutes, then drain.

Combine Everything:

- To serve, transfer rice and lentils to a large serving platter.
- Top with pasta and half of the tomato sauce. Then top with chickpeas and crispy onions for garnish.
- Serve, passing the rest of the sauce and crispy onions separately.

Storage and Leftovers

Refrigeration: *Allow Koshari to cool before transferring to an airtight container. Refrigerate for up to 3–4 days.*
Freezing: *Cool completely, portion into freezer-safe containers, and freeze for 2–3 months.*
Reheating: *Reheat on the stovetop over medium heat or in the microwave, stirring occasionally. For frozen portions, thaw in the fridge overnight and follow stovetop reheating instructions, adding olive oil or water if needed.*

DELICIOUS DESSERTS

'Mantecados' or 'Ghoriba'

Mantecados, also known as Ghoriba, are a cherished North African biscuit, blending Moorish and Spanish culinary traditions. These delicate cookies, with a melt-in-your-mouth texture and delightful flavours, embody centuries of cultural fusion.

Prep time: 15 minutes
Cooking time: 15 minutes
Total time: 30 minutes
Difficulty level: Easy

Ingredients (serves 6-8)

- 500 g of flour or fine semolina
- 250 g sugar
- 250 g vegetable oil
- 1 tsp of baking powder
- Zest of 1 lemon
- Cinnamon or cardamom

How to Prepare

- Preheat the oven to 180ºC.
- In a mixing bowl, combine the flour (or fine semolina), sugar, lemon zest, and oil. Mix well until the dough has a sand-like texture and sticks together.
- Next, form small balls (about the size of a large walnut) and place them on a tray covered with baking paper.
- Then sprinkle some cinnamon (or cardamom) on top of each dough ball.
- Place the biscuits in the oven for 12–15 minutes. Then leave to cool for 10–15 minutes.
- The biscuits must stay white and will harden when cool.
- Serve and enjoy with tea or coffee!

Storage and Leftovers

Refrigeration: *Store in an airtight container in the refrigerator for up to 3–4 days.*
Freezing: *Cool completely, slice into portions, and freeze for up to 2 months.*

Makroud

This mouthwatering North African pastry encapsulates the essence of dates and semolina. Each bite is a journey through the sweet and nutty flavours of this traditional delight, a testament to the rich culinary heritage of the Maghreb region.

Prep Time: 30 minutes
Cook Time: 30 minutes
Total Time: 1 hour
Difficulty: Intermediate

Ingredients (serves 6-8)

For the Syrup:
- 250 ml water
- 400 g sugar
- Juice of 1 lemon

For the Dough:
- 450 g medium semolina
- 130 g plant-based butter (melted)
- 2 tbsp vegetable oil
- 100 ml water
- 35 ml orange blossom water

For the Filling:
- 100 g dates, pitted and chopped (or prepared date paste)
- 1 tsp orange blossom water
- 1 tsp cinnamon

For Frying:
- Vegetable oil

How to Prepare

For the Syrup:
- Prepare sugar syrup by adding water, sugar, and lemon juice in a saucepan. Mix well and bring to a boil. Then reduce heat and simmer for 3–5 minutes, or until sugar is dissolved. Cover to keep warm and runny as you prepare the Makrout.

For the Dough:
- Mix semolina, melted butter, and vegetable oil in a large, wide bowl. Rub the semolina between your hands to work the butter and oil into it, creating a sand-like texture.
- Mix the water and orange blossom water together and gradually add it to the semolina. Knead until the dough comes together.
- Once you have a firm dough, divide it into 3 or 4 smaller portions and roll them into large cylinders.
- Press the middle of the cylinders down using your thumb, creating a sort of tunnel or crevice in the dough cylinders. This is where the date paste will go.

For the Filling:
- Combine chopped dates with orange blossom water and cinnamon to make a thick paste.
- Roll the paste into thin cylinders.

Putting Everything Together:
- Place a portion of the date filling in the centre of the semolina cylinders.
- Enclose the filling with the dough, sealing the edges.
- Roll the combined cylinders to ensure everything is smooth. Make sure no date paste can be seen.
- Cut the cylinders into diamond shapes.

Cooking:

- Fry in vegetable oil until golden brown. Make sure the oil is not too cold or too hot to ensure the Makrouts are cooked through. They should take around 4 minutes each to be fully cooked.
- Once cooked, place in the syrup prepared beforehand and let marinate for around 5 minutes.
- Place onto a serving dish and allow them to cool before serving – they taste great with traditional mint tea.

Storage and Leftovers

Room Temperature: *Store in an airtight container at room temperature for up to 1 week.*

Zalabia

Indulge in the irresistible sweetness of Zalabia, a North African delight that weaves together deep-fried dough soaked in sugar syrup. This delectable treat is a celebration of the region's culinary craftsmanship, offering a delightful blend of textures and flavours.

Prep Time: 15 minutes
Cook Time: 15 minutes
Total Time: 30 minutes
Difficulty: Easy

Ingredients (serves 6-8)

For Sugar Syrup:
- 250 ml water
- 400 g sugar
- Juice of 1 lemon

For Zalabia:
- 250 ml water
- ¾ tbsp of dry yeast
- 1 tsp sugar
- 1 tbsp cornstarch
- 250 g all-purpose flour
- ½ tsp baking powder
- 1 tsp vanilla extract
- ¼ tsp turmeric powder
- Vegetable oil

How to Prepare

- Prepare sugar syrup overnight by adding water, sugar, and lemon juice to a saucepan. Mix well and bring to a boil. Then reduce heat and simmer for 3–5 minutes until sugar is dissolved.
- Mix slightly warm water, yeast, and sugar in a large bowl and leave it to foam up for 2–3 minutes.
- Then add cornstarch, flour, baking powder, vanilla extract, turmeric, and 1 tbsp of oil. Mix thoroughly, then add a bit of water. Keep mixing until you have a thick, smooth paste.
- Let sit and rise for at least 1 hour. Once rested, mix slowly.
- Pour into a squeeze bottle.
- Heat 2 tbsp of oil in a frying pan. Once the oil is hot enough, use the squeeze bottle to create circular designs of the batter.
- Dip the Zalabia in the sugar syrup and put aside after 2–3 minutes of frying, or until light golden brown. Do this until you finish the batter in the squeeze bottle.
- Allow them to cool before serving.

Storage and Leftovers

Room Temperature: *Store in an airtight container at room temperature for up to 3 days.*

LIST OF INGREDIENTS AND UTENSILS

Fruit and Vegetables:

- Apricots
- Aubergine
- Avocado
- Banana
- Bell pepper
- Bitterleaves
- Broccoli
- Cabbage
- Carrots
- Cassava
- Cassava leaves
- Cauliflower
- Celery
- Cherry tomatoes
- Chillies (of choice)
- Courgette
- Cucumber
- Dates
- Garlic
- Lemon
- Lemongrass
- Lime
- Okra
- Olives
- Onion (white and red)
- Plantain (green and ripe)
- Potatoes
- Prunes
- Scotch bonnet pepper
- Spinach
- Spring onion
- Sweet potato
- Tomatoes (large and cherry)
- White cabbage
- Yam

Herbs and Spices:

- Anise (ground)
- Bay leaf
- Berbere spice (1 part of each – dried bird's eye chillies, black pepper, coriander, cumin, cardamom, fenugreek seeds, cloves, salt, smoked paprika, sweet paprika, ginger, cinnamon, and nutmeg)
- Black salt (kala namak)
- Cayenne pepper (ground)
- Chilli flakes
- Chillie powder
- Cinnamon (ground)
- Coriander (fresh and dried)
- Curry powder
- Cumin (ground)
- Dawadawa (African locust beans)
- Fenugreek seeds and powder
- Garlic powder
- Ginger (fresh and ground)
- Hot paprika
- Iru (fermented locust beans)
- Nutmeg (ground)
- Mint (fresh)

- Nori powder (dried mushrooms and nori ground together for a crayfish alternative)
- Oregano
- Parsley (fresh and dried)
- Pepper (ground black)
- Powdered sugar
- Ras el hanout (1 part of each cumin, coriander, cinnamon, ginger, black pepper, turmeric, and cardamom)
- Red African bird-eyes chillies
- Rosemary (sprigs)
- Salt
- Smoked paprika
- Soya pepper
- Sugar
- Sweet paprika
- Thyme (sprigs and dried)
- Turmeric (ground)
- Uziza powder
- White pepper

Grains, Beans, Nuts, and Extras:

- Active dry yeast
- Almond flour
- Almonds
- All-purpose flour
- Baking powder
- Baking soda
- Barley flour
- Black-eye peas
- Breadcrumbs
- Cassava couscous (Attiéké)
- Cassava flour
- Chapati
- Chickpea flour
- Chickpeas
- Cornstarch
- Cornflour
- Desiccated coconut
- Fava beans
- Instant yeast
- Kidney beans
- Lentils
- Melon seeds (ground) for egusi
- Millet couscous
- Pasta (preferably small pasta like macaroni or penne)
- Peanuts (pealed)
- Pistachios
- Pitta
- Rice (any type of choice)
- Rice flour
- Rice paper
- Self-raising flour
- Semolina (fine and medium)
- Sesame seeds
- Sliced bread
- Sorghum and millet grains
- Spring roll or samosa sheets
- Teff flour
- Whole wheat flour
- Yellow split peas

Condiments:

- Apple vinegar
- Apricot jam (or jam of choice)
- Chopped or crushed tomatoes
- Extra virgin olive oil
- Harissa
- Meat-free beef stock cubes
- Miso paste
- Palm nut pulp
- Passata
- Peanut butter
- Peanut oil
- Red palm oil

- Soy sauce
- Tomato paste
- Vanilla extract
- Vegetable broth
- Vegetable oil
- White vinegar

Animal Product Replacements:

- Banana blossom
- Coconut milk
- Extra-firm tofu
- Jackfruit
- King oyster mushroom
- Chestnut mushrooms
- Dried mushrooms
- Nori seaweed sheets
- Oyster mushrooms
- Plant-based butter
- Plant-based double cream
- Plant-based mince (e.g. soy mince)
- Plant-based yoghurt
- Tempeh
- Soy milk

Utensils:

- Aluminium foil
- Ables kiver pan
- Baking paper
- Baking tray
- Blender or food processor
- Chopping board
- Colander
- Couscoussier (a deep saucepan with a steamer that fits on top)
- Fork
- Grater
- Knife
- Ladle
- Large mixing bowl
- Large saucepan with lid
- Long wooden spoon/stick
- Measuring cups and spoons
- Non-stick frying pan with lid
- Paper towels
- Peeler
- Potato masher
- Rolling pin
- Sieve
- Skewers
- Strainer
- Squeeze bottle
- Tablespoons (tbsp)
- Tajine pot
- Teaspoons (tsp)
- Whisk
- Wooden/mixing spoon

ACKNOWLEDGEMENTS

Huge heartfelt appreciation to Susmita, the Global Book Publishing Team, and Thrive Africa for turning our cookbook dreams into a tangible reality.

A special thanks to Dénia Dimsdale for her outstanding contribution to this book. Her unique talent and unwavering commitment have contributed to bringing this project to fruition. This book could never have reached its full potential without her exceptional skills and dedication. A heartfelt thank you for her invaluable and irreplaceable role in making this endeavour a success.

Another very special thanks goes to Kasia Nwansi for her exceptional contributions throughout this project. This book would never have been completed without her exceptional creativity, dedication, attention to detail, and ongoing support. The Pan-African Plant-Based Alliance is eternally grateful for her incredible commitment.

Many thanks to the talented Chisom AmaBertram for her hard work in skilfully capturing the essence of our dishes and for the stunning photography. Her artistry and exceptional creativity have added a vibrant and beautiful dimension to the book.

Lastly, a huge thanks to Alexandra Kotto for her invaluable support. Her guidance, encouragement, and hands-on assistance were instrumental in keeping this project on track.

Finally, we extend our immense gratitude to the incredible African Aunties and Uncles whose expertise and approval elevated and perfected each recipe in this collection.

The creators of this book extend their deepest gratitude to the rich heritage of the African continent and the African diaspora for their unwavering love, boundless joy, and remarkable resilience.

Hotep!

Printed in Great Britain
by Amazon

a20a1996-3408-4af4-9193-3767d1315cb9R01